"Dear Evil Tester"

Alan Richardson

"Dear Evil Tester"

Alan Richardson

This book is for sale at
http://EvilTester.com/DearEvilTester

This version was published on 2016-03-16

ISBN 978-0-9567332-7-6

The right of Alan Richardson to be identified as the author
of this work has been asserted by him in accordance with
the Copyright, Design and Patents Act 1988. The views
expressed in this book are those of the author.

First Published in Great Britain 2016 by Compendium
Developments Ltd (http://www.compendiumdev.co.uk)
contact details: alan@compendiumdev.co.uk

Every effort has been made to ensure that the information contained in this book is accurate at the time of going to press, and the publishers and author cannot accept any responsibility for any errors or omissions, however caused. While the text of this book appears to take the format of 'advice'. No-one in their right mind would accept and implement all the advice written in this book. Indeed the advice is deliberately written to make you think. It is not to be slavishly followed. No responsibility for loss or damage occasioned by any person acting, or refraining from action, as a result of the material in this publication can be accepted by the editor, the publisher or the author.

e-book ISBN : 978-0-9567332-6-9

paper book ISBN : 978-0-9567332-7-6

Contents

CONTENTS

Introduction

One of the great opportunities I had when contributing to "The Testing Planet", was answering people's letters, or in this case 'Questions'. We created a "Dear Evil Tester" column, an obvious rip-off of the Agony Aunt columns that have existed in newspapers for a bazillion years.

I haven't added these to the book in chronological order, I've added them in the order that I think either motivates the reader most, or for comic effect, or I just pasted them in randomly. Whichever explanation works for you is undoubtedly the correct one. If it looks like genius, then I meant it.

In fact the very first one, I made up. Apparently this is common practice in the newspaper industry, but I did it to kickstart the process. You might even be able to tell which letter it is. I know which one it is, but I'm not telling. All the other letters were 'real'.

I had no idea if the people on the receiving end of my advice were serious in their questioning, or if they were contributing to the global joke that was "Dear Evil Tester". Frankly, I didn't care. I always planned to take their question seriously and produced a serious answer injected with all the humour, scorn, and cynicism I could muster. Additionally, lacing the answer with the 'I wish someone had told me this when I was younger' attitude that I wanted out there in the testing community.

A Book of Three Halves

This is a book of two halves, and an extra bit. The first section contains the 'published' letters and answers. This is a nice, fun, gentle introduction to the world of the Evil Tester.

The second half is darker, harder, at times intensely practical, but still edgy advice. The kind of advice you don't receive anywhere else, possibly for good reason.

And then we finish with some essays which summarise the attitudes and approaches evidenced in the letter answers.

So prepare yourself. If you are just here for a good time, then forget it, you're going to learn stuff as well and be pushed to think about what you do.

On Publishing

I was somewhat reticent in publishing this. After all "Evil Tester" is a persona, not me, and while sometimes I channel him to make a point, or to rail at the world, he doesn't represent my normal communication approach.

Frankly I was worried that some people would never speak to me again. I've forgotten who most of the people submitting questions were, if I ever knew, but I'm sure I recognise some of them. And some of them I hope will speak to me again.

Also, I'm not sure how the world of work will react to this, some people might never employ me after reading this. But then, some people will never employ me anyway.

And I'm sure you, dear reader, don't care about my employment prospects. After all, when one writes a book one instantly becomes rich and famous.

Also, you may not have even paid for this book, you might have ripped it off some torrent or something (if you did and they embedded a virus in the middle then don't blame me). If you did pay for it, then thank you. I do hope it entertains you, perhaps you'd consider employing me as a consultant as well?

And I know some of you don't care about my employment prospects given the advice I received from some of you:

- "You should swear more"
  - I'm pretty sure I don't swear at all in here. After all, we are gentlefolk. And if it's in the dictionary, I'm pretty sure that doesn't count as swearing. And worry not for I don't even use those words, so all the little children here, you can read this text without any fear.
- "You should write more strongly"
  - While touchtyping does make my fingers stronger, I'm not prepared to bench press solely using them. I think that is why God invented arms. That, and to make it easier to peel bananas.
- "You should name and shame"

- – I put my name on the cover. Oh, the shame I feel.
- "Make a stand. Take a single position."
    - – The only principle I'm prepared to absolutely commit to, with absolute certainty, is that I can change my mind.
- "Add more facts"
    - – If I add a fact in here, people might think it is made up. Then where would they be. They'd start believing made up facts and figures thinking they were real because they read it in black and white in a book and books deal with facts don't they. If you don't believe me read Robert Anton Wilson's Illuminatus books, then try and work out what is fact and what is fiction.

And frankly some of you are my competitors. We work in the same industry. We do similar things. And if I become unemployable then that works in your favour. I'm not going to be cynical and attribute this motivation to everyone that encouraged me. Of course I can think of someone who did, and might have, but... I'm sure they didn't, well, I'm mostly sure.

On Formatting

Some of you may notice that your name, no longer has its special characters in it. Yup, that was me. I took them out. Sorry. I didn't fancy maintaining anything except ZX81 alpha chars. Feel free to write to someone else and complain.

When I started writing this book I originally formatted the 'letters' as:

Dear Evil Tester,

blah blah blah

from,

Someone

But, honestly, that seemed like padding. So I've done the decent thing and removed most of the formatting so now they look like this:

❓ blah blah blah, blah de blah blah, blah de blah de blah, blah, de blah de blah blah?

Someone very special

Then my answer in here.

Periodically there might even be a commentary

If I do write a commentary, then it will look like this.

It may not read like a letter, but at least you can take the consolation to heart that I don't want to rip you off with an inflated page count.

Nope, no padding in here. Every word I write has value. I don't just put text in here to up the word count and increase the number of pages so that you believe you have a bigger bundle of pages than you actually do. I would not do that to you. Take me at my word that I consider your decision to purchase this book as incredibly important to me and I would do nothing that might damage that trust between us, so you will not find any artificial padding in here.

Nope, none.

Nada, never ever.

That's right, not... ever.

Enjoy.

Slogans! Slogans! We don't need no stinkin' slogans

You might even see slogans. These are designed to motivate, provoke, make you laugh, make you cry. Actually most of these Eviltesterisms are generated randomly by "The Eviltestersloganiser" (and yes, that is me too).

Acknowledgements

I am grateful to everyone that submitted questions. I'd mention you all by name but we anonymized you for publication and review. After all, it's an agony aunt column. You bared your soul to the world, and I mocked you for it.

Thank you all. I'm sure I could have made up questions, but they would not have provided the ring of truth that your true life painful experiences did.

Also thanks to the folks involved in the publication of some of these answers in the Testing Planet.

Those of you I know were involved by name:

- Rob Lambert
    - Rob was the first editor of the Testing Planet who introduced "Dear Evil Tester" as a regular feature and promoted it so well that we had 'real' reader's questions. A miracle. Thanks for laughing at my early drafts and tightening up the writing. I used my drafts in this book to avoid your heavy handed censorship and more professionally edited and tightly written prose.
- Rosie Sherry
    - Rosie took the risk of publishing this nonsense in the paper. I have no idea of the critical

ix

reception because she shielded me from such fame and fortune. Thanks also for creating the Politically Correct iconography for Evil Tester rather than my crudely scribbled drawing. I have used my scribbles in this book to add an authentic homespun charm to the proceedings, and to avoid any licensing fees.

- Simon Knight
  - Simon for carrying on Rob's torch, excellent editing, and gathering many more questions for the answering.

And I'm sure there were other Testing Planet people involved. You all did a great job.

Thank you to the reviewers who provided comments that I fed into the editing process, and who also kindly provided testimonial blurbs that I could butcher for promotional purposes: Gojko Adzic, Richard Bradshaw, Paul Gerrard, Andy Glover, Dorothy Graham, Rob Lambert, James Lyndsay, Rob Sabourin, Huib Schoots.

Any remaining errors are mine, and either intentional, or due to my poor grammar skills. You can decide. And remember, I do so enjoy starting sentences with a conjunction. And writing partial sentences[1]. Stop reading now if you can't handle it.

---

[1]I'd love to claim that this style was deliberate and influenced by my study of pulp novels from the 30's and 40's, but I suspect it stems from my inability to read my English teacher's handwritten comments on my school homework.

Thanks also to my family: Billie and Keeran, for putting up with my answers to their questions. The quality of the answers you read here is representative of the quality of answers they receive at home. Just imagine how badly my answers impact my son's homework.

And thanks to you, dear reader, for joining us.

Welcome to the World of "Dear Evil Tester"

You can still ask me anything

If you have any questions you would like to see in a future volume then please let me know:

- www.eviltester.com/askmeanything[2]

The "Dear Evil Tester" Letters

The hardest part of coming up with the answers was what to sign off as.

Should it be E, or Uncle E, or Auntie Evil, etc. etc.

You can see the range of titles I used.

If you have a favourite then feel free to adopt it as your email signature, I won't charge you.

 **Of course I'm not Evil...
Do I look Evil?**

Are you truly evil?

 Are you truly evil or just misunderstood?
Vernon

Dear Vernon,

Probably neither.

In an attempt to make this section more interactive I offer you more options.

Could it be:

1. I'm deliberately engaging in false advertising for shock effect.
2. I can't spell. I meant to write "live" tester, incorrectly wrote it as "vile" tester and hastily corrected it to "evil" tester. And now I have to live with this vile tag forever. Poor poor pitiful me.
3. I got drunk and, well... you know how it goes.
4. *insert your plausible answer here*

E.

When is testing not required?

 When can a person say that testing is not required for a particular product ?

Yogesh

Hi Yogesh,

I like questions with flippant answers. So, of course the answer is "Whenever they want". They can equally say "Bibble Bibble" whenever they want.

But I suspect you want a less flippant and more scientific answer (Bwahaha).

My first Google search for "% of IT projects that fail" provided me with a scientific range of "62 - 68"%. I will make this complicated statistic easy for my readers by conclusively stating that 70% of IT projects fail.

Therefore, I can conclude that 100% of people on 70% of IT projects can say "Testing is not required for this particular product" and they can hold their heads up high in the hope that the project was doomed anyway. Pretty good odds.

Consequently we only have to concern ourselves with the 100% of people involved in 30% of IT projects.

We all know that "you can't test quality into a product" therefore I can use this to conclude that the product will either be quality or it won't, so we can't use 'quality' as a justification for testing.

So basing my judgement on the preceding science; I can say: if a person has the power to cause the project to fail, then they can say "testing is not required", at the point they make the decision to doom the project.

Making rocket science look easy,

Oncle E.

 ## Are you a good little tester?

Don't patronize me, I'm not a good little tester!

I'm better than that. I'm Eeevil.

Why are you evil?

 Why are you evil?

George

Hi George,

Thanks for asking. Its not often people ask that. Actually they do. And I give lots of answers. So here is one. Ask again and you might get another.

Testers very often don't think that they can go beyond the norms.

They think they need permission.

The point is we don't need permission.

We should do whatever it takes.

We should be using the system as a system. We should manipulate it.

It is one of the few things that we can manipulate without consequence, without worrying about its feelings. We can do whatever we want to it. We can act however we need to, to fulfil our part in the project.

We have to do things to the system that no-one else will do.

Things that no one else is *prepared* to do.

Things that no-one else can even conceptualise that it is something that you would ever want to do.

I use the term "Evil", to give me the freedom and flexibility to do that.

Hope that helps,

Cap'n E of the Good Ship 'vil

PS. Do whatever it takes.

PPS. You can tell your boss I said so.

OK, so I cheated.

"What so early in the book?"

Yup, that's what testers try to do. We cheat. Get over it.

I was asked this question after a keynote session in Poland at "Agile Testing and Automation".

But I liked the answer and wanted to share it with you.

What is the most evil metric?

 What is the most evil metric that is used in software testing, and did you invent it?

Steve

Dear Steve,

Any metric can be used to beat people over the head. Much malfeasance can be done in their name.

"Number of Test Cases" ranks high on the twisted scale because, even when not wielded, simply gazing upon it, casts a spell of malevolence.

Consider. One has to posit the existence of a tangible physical entity called a 'Test Case' before one can even make sense of the words. This immediately puts the innocent reader in a state where such terrible things can become manifest in this world.

Most testers have not read the "Experior Maleficarum", they have not learned to recognise 'words of disreputable definition', and even an Indagator trained in the "Rituale Exploro" can lapse when confronted with primitive heathen words of power such as this.

As soon as one posits the existence of a test case it becomes natural to ask questions such as "how many do we need?" And worse, "how many have you done?"

And then you start to think you haven't done enough, given how many you need to do. And how you do you increase the "Number of Test Cases" done? By making it possible to 'do' them faster, by associating each counted 'Test Case' with a 'Test Script' - this allows you to add cheaper and more 'Unskilled Testers' to the project to transmute ever more 'Test Cases' into the noble "Done Test".

And as we all know, once a 'Test Case' is done, it can never be undone. Otherwise your 'test coverage' metric and 'test progress against estimate' metrics become invalid. Therefore we restrict the validity to the phase within which they transmute.

And so we see that a simple four word invocation leads to the primitive constructs which once were used in the savage times including "Test Phase", "Test Scripts", "Unskilled Tester" "Pass/Fail".

Brrr, I get chills just thinking about it.

I did not invent this metric. I confess, I have used it, but I didn't inhale,

Frater Evil

Evil Tester and the Agile Team

Any tips for a certification exam?

 Do you have any tips on taking the {insert nominated certification board name here} certification exam?

Anon

Dear Anon,

Why yes I do. And I will not say "do not take it". It is your money, consequently, your choice.

I, for example, once bought an expensive jacket with sleeves that were too short, I still wear it, to remind myself that I should spend my money more wisely and buy jackets with longer sleeves. We all spend our money on daft things every so often, so don't feel bad about that; or do, I don't mind.

Keep to the syllabus. These exams are not like school exams, they want you to pass. After all, you paid for training, if you fail, it makes the trainers look bad, they don't want that. Stick to the syllabus like a piece of discarded chewing gum.

Parrot like an African Grey. Your job, when sitting the exam, is not to display learning, your job is to regurgitate whatever you were told or read in the syllabus. Regardless of what you think about what you were told, your job is to repeat it back.

For multiple choice: don't think "what is the right answer?", instead think "what do *they* think is the right answer?". And watch out for double negatives in questions, these are a useful lazy way of writing questions that trip people up.

For written questions you need to remember that the markers use a set of guidelines. These guidelines tell the marker what type of phrases to expect to see and how many marks to give for each phrase. I harnessed this at university by running through the paper very quickly, regurgitating and parroting words and phrases from the syllabus in the form of a mind-map or outline for each question. If you don't score it out, it becomes part of your answer. Then I would come back later and finish the answer with written English, knowing that I had probably already met the marking guidelines with the brain dump and that I could not run out of time.

You paid. They want to pass you. Make it easy for them to pass you. Write down clearly and concisely whatever it was they told you. Engage your memory, not your brain.

Yours Educashunaly,

Professor Evil

PS. And write with good penmanship. I have marked written answers, and could not understand why one candidate kept writing about "Chicken Feet". To this day, I still don't know what they were trying to write.

If all testing is exploratory, am I no longer special?

 I have always tried to do Exploratory Testing, and felt that that made me special. Now I have heard someone say that all testing is exploratory. Am I really not special at all, after all?

Steven

Dear Steven,

Ah, yes. It is hard when life slams our face into the pavement of reality.

If you want to remain special, like me, then you have to stop listening to other people, like me.

I like to use child logic on arguments that I want to treat as specious. Allow me to help you.

I suspect that the definition of Exploratory Testing they use, includes the null state. Then, even when the testing in question involves no exploration, it still involves exploration - it involves null exploration.

You simply need to use a new, and more complicated scale, one designed to allow you to hang on to your delusion of specialness. I like to call this the 'better', or 'best', scale.

Immediately discard the notion of null exploration as valid. You need to remove that if you want to be judgemental.

I suggest initially setting your "fully exploratory" scale at 20%. Where 20% of testing is exploratory and 80% is not.

Immediately you have become special again. And you have invoked the 80-20 rule, allowing you to make a pretence of scientific categorisation.

Then it becomes a simple matter of adding more grades in your scale to help you further label the testing of other people.

There is one special step that I like to take. Enumerate everything that you do, and only you do, and then define 'true' Exploratory Testing as the specific combination of items that you enumerated. Then you not only cease 'trying' to do Exploratory Testing, you become the only person doing it. And that will make you really special.

Helping peel faces off pavements since 2011,

Auntie Evil

 **I'm not evil, I'm just doing WHATEVER it takes**

How can I get involved at the requirements stage?

 How can I convince my managers to let me get involved and begin testing at the requirement stage?

Soz

Dear Soz,

Hmmm. There are a lot of ways to do this. The testing industry has been building up a lot of material and books and standards and processes for years that cover this very topic.

Sadly, I'm not going to encourage you with their reasons because I think that most of that material presents 'testing' as: "start spending 100% of my time on the project, formally writing a test strategy, approach, and plan, and writing test cases and scripts which are cross referenced to the requirements, even though the requirements are changing and therefore much of the 'testing' would lead to waste and rework".

I've done this myself. I had to do a lot of rework, and saw a lot of waste. I don't want to see you do that to yourself.

Do you think your managers hear you asking to be allowed to do that?

If I was your manager I would want to know: What value will you add? How much time do you think you need to spend? What risks are there to the project, if you are not involved now? How will your involvement in this new project impact your current project? What do you think you would produce as a result of your involvement? What is the risk of rework to the products you will produce over this time? How will it benefit the future of the project for you to be involved?

But beware. If they let you in, then you have the responsibility of demonstrating that you can add value early in the project.

And if that statement has you provoked you into a rant; "How dare he question my ability! Why I can add value easily by ..." Then verbalise your rant to them.

If you can convince people that your involvement will add value, then if they are good, and if they are in control of the process, then they will let you add that value.

Just make sure you avoid waste,

Cuddly Uncle Evil

Evil Tester and the Strategy to buy more time

Can I make a decent living as a tester?

 Can I make a decent living as a freelance tester?

Paul

Hi Paul,

If by freelance you mean, just randomly testing things and submitting bug reports and hoping to be paid for them. Then, no, no I don't think you can. Although if you figure out how to, then please let me know as I'd like to follow your example.

If you mean, work as a contract tester where someone hires you to test stuff on a contractual basis, then yes, some people do manage to make a decent living as a contractor who tests.

The best way I know to get started is to make sure your skills are honed and in demand. Market yourself effectively in your CV and create a web presence to elevate you above most of the people applying for work. Interview well and honestly, and when you work, add value to the workplace.

Fear not though.

Even if you currently can't do the things above, there are enough ineffective hiring managers around, such that you can make a decent living from creating a fake CV, lying about having a bunch of in vogue certifications, and exaggerating your experience. You might not enjoy the end result though.

Yours,

Career Officer Evil

PS. I'm not currently hiring.

 Be the "E" word.

How do you deal with a developer with attitude?

 How must a tester deal with a developer, especially when the developer carries the attitude that he is always right?

Baz

Hi Baz,

I have similar problems. Since I too am always right I occasionally butt heads with a misguided developer who thinks that they are more right than me.

If you are 100% sure that they are not right, and have evidence, then let the evidence speak for itself. Of course the evidence may have to speak to the developer's manager since the developer can always block out the evidence through clever selective listening.

Sometimes I find it useful to compromise. Let them win half the argument, wait till they've fixed half of what you want. Then start up the argument later and fight for the second half.

Sometimes I listen to the developer, and sometimes when I do that I find myself being influenced by their argument, because sometimes they are not wrong. (I hate it when this happens.)

I've always liked these words "The Gestalt Prayer[3]" by Fritz Perls from "Gestalt Therapy Verbatim" and when I remember them, they help me.

I do my thing and you do your thing.
I am not in this world to live up to your expectations,
And you are not in this world to live up to mine.
You are you, and I am I,
and if by chance we find each other, it's beautiful.
If not, it can't be helped.

Hope that helps,

Team Dynamics Therapist Evil

---

[3]https://en.wikipedia.org/wiki/Gestalt_prayer

Pinnocchio's nose?

If Pinocchio were to say "My nose will grow now", what would happen?

James

Dear James,

Ah, philosophy involving an impertinent nose.

Fortunately for me, Pinocchio's reaction is physiological rather than philosophical. A curious thing though. Pinocchio's nose grows when he experiences cognitive dissonance and, when he knowingly and maliciously tells a lie, but... "Unluckily, in a Marionette's life there's always a BUT which is apt to spoil everything." But, not always, because we know that Pinocchio's nose does not grow when he lies if he lies because he is too embarrassed to admit the truth.

Because we testers are versed in the arts of System Thinking and Modelling, we would model Pinocchio as a complex and probabilistic system. With Pinocchio's nose as one system, having a homoeostatic relationship to the system of a living wooden doll.

Also, in our reading of Pinocchio we see that he takes no pleasure in the growing of his nose and is normally embarrassed by it, so probably I think, his nose would not grow.

A counter question to you dear reader. If Pinocchio were an experienced test manager and he wrote in a test strategy "Testing will demonstrate that the system is fit for purpose to go live". Would his nose grow?

Yours, physiologically incapable of performing philosophy,

Uncle E

Evil Testing Skill Set

How do you deal with a tester not pulling their weight?

 What's the best way to deal with a fellow tester who is not pulling his/her weight?

Anon

Dear Anon,

The 'best' way. I don't know. My advice isn't usually 'best'.

And I don't normally do manual labour so this is a very tricky question to answer.

I have been a manager though. And I have seen unbalanced teams where some testers appear to be doing more work than others.

My first step is to check my observation. I investigate if the person is actually under performing. Sometimes they are performing differently and the observations we are making don't include all the work they are doing. Generally I follow Deming's advice and try to change the system to help prevent such misunderstandings, or change the system so that under-performance is shown clearly.

Your question suggests that the tester in question is a peer, rather than someone you manage. So you may not be in full possession of the facts relating to your peer.

My advice to you is to raise your concerns to your manager, after all your lazy manager usually has plenty of time on their hands, and it is their responsibility to deal with your light-weight under performing co-workers.

Yours,

Team Spirit Coach Evil

Tools make everything easier

 I'm not good. I'm better than that.

Why is database testing painful?

 Why is database testing so painful?

Mike

Dear Mike,

Are you confusing database testing with physical torture?

If so, then you'll want to read my "Evil Tester's Handy Tips Summary Guide to Telling The Difference Between Physical Torture and Database Testing" below.

In database testing we tend to do some, or all, of the following:

- insert data into a set of tables
- delete records when the system isn't expecting it
- generate data randomly using an automated tool
- stress the database with 1000s of transactions
- use powerful Extract, Transform and Load (ETL) tools on the database

Please don't confuse the above with actions on your own person, so for a pain free testing experience, never do any, or all, of the following:

- insert anything into yourself at work

- ask people to steal your chair when you try to sit down
- create a machine to randomly shoot cutlery at you
- ask your team to help you run the gauntlet
- use power tools on yourself

Don't worry Mike, we've all been there. I've still got the scars to prove it. But by following my handy tips above I'm sure you'll start to find database testing less painful.

Yours,

Auntie Evel

 Joke Time

Question: Where do testers sit in an organisation?

Answer: On bean bugs!

Should I pretend to test?

 In the past I have worked with project managers who have only pretended to manage. Just in case I come across this sort again in the future, I want to know; should I only pretend to test too, as a form of self-preservation?

Eliza

Dear Eliza,

Ah, a philosophy question.

How do you know you don't already 'pretend' to test? What does it mean to 'really' test something?

But since I don't do philosophy. I can answer simply.

"NO".

If you short change yourself then that isn't self-preservation. It is allowing your skills and integrity to slowly rot, wither and die. It is condemning yourself to victimhood as a response to other people's actions. Don't do that to yourself.

Always. Always. Work to the highest level that you can be proud of. That is an act of self-preservation. That is a process of self-maintenance. That is a coping strategy which allows you to weather the storms of incredulity that attempt to swamp you on project after project.

I try very hard to get in the habit of evaluating myself. Not in terms of the actions of others, or in terms of their expectations of me, or in terms of a 'generic' tester. I try to evaluate myself in terms of my expectations of me. And I try to continually raise my expectations.

I'm not going to tell you to stop evaluating people and building perceptions of them, because that is an essential skill to office survival. We have to learn who the predators are so that we either keep our distance from them, or hunt them in a pack.

All the best,

Uncle Evil

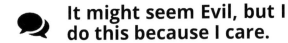 **It might seem Evil, but I do this because I care.**

Should developers do eunuch testing?

 What's all this I hear about how developers should do eunuch testing?

Jim

Dear Jim,

I can't tell if it is your hearing, or your reading, that is at fault.

If it is your hearing then you have misheard the word "unit". Unit testing is where developers test an individual thing. For example, if I was a developer and I had just written a system, then that system is an individual thing. So I (as a developer) have to write what is known as a "Unit" test, i.e. an individual test. So I write a single test to cover my entire system as a Unit.

This has now evolved in Agile projects into an advanced process called TDD or Test Driven Development.

In TDD testers are given complete control over the project and drive it to completion, which they do by shouting at the developers as they sprint around the room. They typically shout things like "Now write a failing test", "Check your style", "Refactor it into your poker" and other suitably motivating slogans.

If it is your reading at fault then you probably mean "enough" testing. And as we know, there is no such thing as "enough" testing.

And how do we know?

Because asking "How much testing is enough?" is like asking "How long is a piece of string?".

As an example, I have a piece of string on my desk, it is 302 mm long. And it isn't long enough.

Hope this helps you in your next stand up meeting,

Uncle E

 I'm not laughing 'at' you.

How do you prevent boredom?

 How do you prevent boredom while retesting and ensure that you are always eager
to break the tested product as you were the
first day you got the product?

Sowa

Dear Sowa,

It might sound glib, but my immediate response is to say
"Stop doing the same things you did on the first day."

I must have a different attitude though, as I don't really
understand your situation. If someone gives you something
and asks you to test it again and again and again. How do
your eyes not fire up? How does your trident not tingle
with delight? How can you not be eager to test? How is
that possible?

The only time I don't feel that way is when I'm using
software that I need. For example, I'm real careful when
I use bank automated teller machines. A life lesson that
cost me 50 Great British Pounds when I couldn't afford it.
True story, don't ask, the memories still pain me to this day.
When I'm using, I try very hard not to trigger problems.

When I'm testing. I'm not using.

But as to how? I'll tell thou, now. And this time I'll do it in
rhyme. Because to not do so... would be a crime.

Ahem...

As if it were the first day

Testing's not besting the code they produce,
We work hard and challenge ourselves to deduce
Ever more interesting ways that we might
Have deluded ourselves into thinking "everything's right".

If we ever glaze over and stop observing anew
We'll miss bugs by the dozen not by the one or the two.

So partly it's fear that keeps me in focus,
Fear that somebody else will notice,
That tiny small thing of no real consequence
"How did I miss it, it makes no sense!"

There's no time like the past. To experience time is illusion
There's no time like the present, so I have a solution.

I stay in the now, but not in the zone,
I stay alert, with intent, and I'm not alone.
All of my skills, and my models and all of my tools,
The software can't win. I have no other rules.

I never re-test. I test and I test and I test and I test.
And now, again, as if for the first time, I will test it the best

---

May all your good testing dreams come true,

All @ EvilTester.com

How do you define concurrent users?

 Why is there so much argument about the definition of "concurrent users" in performance testing?

Mark

Dear Mark,

The argument stems from the belief that people can't multi-task, so the notion of a concurrent user makes no sense to some people.

It remains my fervent belief that this argument would not take place if everyone learned how to juggle.

Hope that helps you in your next non-functional requirements meeting,

All @ EvilTester.com

 If someone left a door open, would you walk in? Of course you would.

How do I gain the respect of developers?

 I want my developers to respect me and the work I do. I've tried learning the programming language they use but this takes time and effort. What's the easiest and/or quickest way to gain respect as a tester?

Andi

Dear Andi,

Thanks for asking this really important question. In fact it's so important I'm honestly going to give you real tools to deal with this situation. No joking around. No messing about. This answer provides "therapy on a stick" for the common tester.

I've heard the 'respect' cry since I started testing. I still hear this type of question asked at conferences and testing events so I'm sure plenty of testers are reading your question and nodding along. "Yup, I don't get none of that necessary respectful neither".

I too found myself caught up in that tester hysteria. I felt the way I imagine you might be feeling now. Poor poor pitiful me.

But I got over it. I gave myself a healthy dose of sane juice to stop that delusional thinking.

You can too.

But before I explain how, I need to mock you a little first. I don't want to mock you, but it's mandatory. I don't enjoy mocking you, but I took an oath. Claiming 'respect' victim status means that I have to trigger your self-respect defence mechanisms.

Think. Now. Have you got a skill? Any skill?

When someone comes up to you and says "Hey, I tried to learn your skill but I found it quite hard, it took too much time and effort so I stopped - do you respect me more now?"

What's your first instinct?

And mind your language.

Stop using that word. 'Respect' is a woolly, ambiguous word. It spans the spectrum from "being nice" to "I'm almost in awe". You don't mean it. You don't want it.

Are you ready to defend yourself and tell me how my behaviour showed evidence of a lack of respect? Ready to tell me what you want me to do differently next time?

[wannabe life coaches note the use of provocation as a therapeutic tool]

And now. How?

How do you know they don't respect you? Did you ask them? "Do you respect me?" Did they say "No"? Ignore their answer, you'd still be no closer to your 'quick fix'.

The person you really need to ask is... you.

How do you know they don't respect you? What, in their behaviour, do you use as the evidence that allows you to maintain the belief that they don't respect you?

That behaviour, or absence of behaviour, gives you an actionable request you can make of them, or work with them to prevent happening.

If you know they don't respect you because... say... they don't invite you to the planning meetings, then you can say "I'd like to be invited to the planning meeting because then I'll know what's coming and can identify spiffingly splendid risks in advance".

[Note: It doesn't really matter what you say as a 'because'. You can get all tautological on them "... because then I can attend the planning meeting". Cialdini provides examples, in "Influence - science and practice", that 'Influence' doesn't require a good reason, it just requires a reason.]

They might say "Oh, we didn't invite you to those because we thought the work you're doing was so important that we didn't want to waste your time." And then you know that you were delusional all along, and I saved you a small fortune on therapy.

Of course they might not. In which case, as well as asking myself "How?" I'll point out that I also learned how to juggle. Nothing pulls in the respect dollar like a good three ball clawed hand cascade.

Don't worry about payment, your tears of gratitude are payment enough.

All @ EvilTester.com

PS. always assume tears stem from gratitude.

PPS. delusions should help us not hinder us.

Can't juggle? No Problem.
Just throw lots of balls in
the air and take a photo.
It's easier.

My team only cares about defects, what do I do?

 My team only seems to care about defects, they don't seem to care about testing, what should I do?

Earnest

Dear Earnest,

Yeah that happens. You spend all that time writing test cases and scripts and producing a big test plan (that they still haven't signed off!) And then all they care about are results! Well they count it as results, you count it as one of your many valuable outputs. And if you spend all your time raising defects you'll never get any testing done.

Its a strange life we testers lead. Defects stop us achieving coverage. Coverage leads to more (and presumably 'better' testing) and yet people only care about bugs.

Well here's what you could do. Yes, I don't recommend this. And yes I haven't tried this. But hey - you caught me in a good mood. So I'll tell ya.

Options:

- a) Buy lots of bugs, you know those creepy crawly, 6, 7, 8, 9, 100 legged beasty things, and just leave them running about the office and see how they like them apples.

- b) Find an open-source project's bug database and just screen scrape the defects into your tracking system - Bam! Hundreds of defects from one automated script (see, learning how to automate has its uses).
- c) Just keep raising the same defect over and over again. At least this way you can tell if they're even reading the things!

Ha. But of course I'm just kidding. They are all ridiculous suggestions.

So seriously now...

In the testing world people spend a lot of time talking about metaphors, and heuristics, and similes, and analogies. You know stuff that is like the thing, but is not the thing, but seems like the thing, and reminds you of the thing in ways that the thing is kind of like but isn't. Stuff that triggers thinking and imagineering but isn't really test design, you know, that voodoo hoodoo testy magic stuff that *they* talk about but isn't *real* test design. Yeah. Yeah. You with me. Yeah sister.

So how does that help you here.

Well.

You know how people go on, and on, about requirements. And how the software has to do all the stuff that the user wants. And requirements are supposed to represent what the user wants. But when you implement the requirement and the user sees it and they are all like "hey what is this" and all "I don't like this" yeah, and even "I didn't say that, who said I said that, did you add that one when I wasn't looking, who signed these off" etc. etc. etc. (But we all know how much fun it is to sneak those extra requirements in, so we don't want to stop doing that, otherwise software development just wouldn't be fun any more.)

So really, we could think of requirements as metaphors or similes, you know, then Dev Teams can riff off them to come up with software that is kinda like the requirement, so it might come close to filling the user's need, without all the hassle of really dealing with the requirements, which let's face it, they don't know anyway.

Well we can do that too, to find bugs.

So. Here's what you do.

Pick some software, any software. Say, oh I don't know... a search engine. And let's say you're testing a, oh I don't know... an accounting package.

Well what you do is look at the functionality of the search engine, identify all the functionality in that, and then try and do the same stuff in the accounting package that you are supposed to be testing. And if your accounting package doesn't do the thing- hey, you just found a defect.

So try and search for "evil tester" in your accounting package and see how far that gets you. It didn't work! Bug.

Type in "evil" and look for the quick tip completion drop down. What, it didn't appear! Bug.

Try and click on the "I feel lucky" button in your accounting software. What, you can't find it! Bug.

See - three bugs in 30 seconds. And you could keep going, just look for another piece of software and map it on to yours. Bug. Bug. Bug.

Of course you'll get the normal objections from the dev team: "The requirements don't say that!" "The user would never do that!" "It works on my machine!" But hey, you've heard those excuses before, they won't stop you. Keep going. Your bug count goes up and up and up.

And that was what they wanted! Right!

Great - go do it.

Warning: this might get you fired

Warning: this really is a valid technique for coming up with test ideas, I might have just twisted it a little

Buy hey, go do... testy stuff

Hope that helps with your problem Earnest,

Yours sincerely, all the best, hugs and kisses, etc. etc. from all @ EvilTester.com

Unpublished Questions

Yes, you read this correctly. The Unpublished Questions.

The stuff that didn't get published.

The questions I never got around to finishing writing the answers to.

The answers that were too shocking to ever appear in print before now.

Welcome to 'The Vault of Unpublished Questions'.

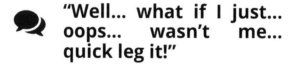 **"Well... what if I just... oops... wasn't me... quick leg it!"**

How to track Exploratory Testing?

Dear Evil Tester,

My question is about exploratory testing tools. Do you recommend any tools for note-taking and managing test sessions? I'm looking for something easy to use and able to share sessions with other people. Something that developers would like to use because developers do testing in my company. Our stack is JavaScript and some PHP and we're working on MacBooks. All Java-like tools wouldn't be desirable.

I think I heard your recommendation for Evernote. Do you really recommend that? Kaz

Hi Kaz,

Thanks for asking.

I have tried lots of tools over the years and I personally now use the simplest tools I can.

That way I always have access to them, or a variant of them, on any machine that I test on.

The simplest tool I have found is...

Wait for it.

A text editor.

Yup, my universal solution now, is a text editor.

And here's the really cool thing. Developers love text editors. Particularly when they are doing dynamic languages.

You could use Sublime Text - that's cool. (Even cooler if you spring for the registration fee to use it legally.) Or you could go all cutting edge with Atom. (Both cross platform and non-Java so you won't get banished.)

If you are hardcore then you can turn to Vim or Emacs. But that is way out of my league. I like my editors simple.

This works for me, when I perform Exploratory Testing, because I make my notes serially. Top to bottom, start to finish.

I add timestamps in my notes to track time.

I write things like:

```
1   ## Jira123
2
3   10:10 Starting to test Jira123
```

The above would be in a file called `20151119_0900.txt`

Because my day started at `09:00` on the `19th of November 2015`.

And I do use Evernote as well. I'll often paste between Evernote and a text editor because Evernote syncs between different machines, so I can start testing on the Windows machine, and continue testing on the Mac with access to the same notes. When I use Evernote I create a note called '20151119 Daily Notes'. I can import and export from Evernote from the text editors so I move back and forth between them. I often work with Evernote because I can paste in screenshots directly.

When I work with text editors I have to write in the name of the file to which I saved the screenshot.

I tend to use Markdown as my formatting in my text editing. Because if I want to make it pretty I can use dillinger.io[4], or Pandoc[5], or stackedit.io[6], etc.

So yes, I use Evernote and text editors for taking my notes.

When working with a team we then need to add a tracking layer. So I tend to version control my raw notes and screen shots. e.g. folder structure:

```
1   - alan
2     - 2015
3       - 11_November
4         - 19
5           - images
6             - loginScreenError_0930.png
7           - misc
8           20151119_0900.txt
```

The above could all be version controlled.

---

[4]http://dillinger.io
[5]http://pandoc.org
[6]http://stackedit.io

I try to use the tracking tools that are used on the project.

For example: If we are using Jira then I would have a task for each of my testing sessions and I would create a text file for each session. I would then copy and paste from my raw notes, into the Jira task that was tracking my testing.

That way I have raw notes that support my testing process on disk, and version control, and in Evernote for easy searching. And I have the formal tracking notes in the tracking system.

This tends to work because I mainly operate on Agile projects where 'Story' is the entity that we track work against.

We have in the past, also used wiki's to share notes, and I can just copy paste information from my text notes to persist them in the wiki. In this instance I write in Wiki Markup rather than Markdown.

I aim to report using the existing project reporting tools and build my test reporting approach around those.

Does that help?

Hopefully it gives you some ideas. But take away the ultimate guiding principle.

Keep it simple soldier. Because that's what we do, fight the good fight.

Signing off,

Sergeant EEEEEEEEvil!

Evil Tester and The Progress Report

What is Exploratory Testing?

 Yo E! What is Exploratory Testing?
Rich

Dear Rich,

I used to go exploring as a child. Out in the woods and over the fields. And when we came back we had had numerous adventures, found lots of cool stuff and done lots of cool things. But when asked, I couldn't remember all of the cool things, and I couldn't remember exactly where I'd been, nor how long I'd been out. I wasn't really exploring. I was playing. Our intent, as children, was to have fun. We just called it 'exploring'.

I used to go Exploratory Testing early in my learning. I found lots of cool bugs, used lots of cool tools and tried lots of cool things. But when asked, I couldn't remember all the cool things, or why I had tried them. I couldn't remember exactly where in the system I'd been, nor how long I'd been testing. I wasn't really exploring. I was playing. But my intent was Exploratory Testing, I hadn't understood what that meant.

I don't particularly like definitions. I do however like descriptions. And when I describe Exploratory Testing, I try to include the notion of intent, or deliberateness, or purpose.

I consider intent one of the key concepts which nudges my testing in the direction of professionalism, or not.

The discussions over the years for Exploratory Testing have resulted in a number of obvious places where 'intent' manifests.

- Missions
- Charters
- Questions
- Risks
- Notes
- Reports
- Debriefs

These are places where we reveal our high level intentions towards the software. These are the easiest forms of intent to incorporate into your Exploratory Testing process.

If you don't do this already, then start now.

Test with intent, with minimal up front planning, taking responsibility for your path and the communication of your journey.

If you do that, then I think you'll increase your chances of identifying what Exploratory Testing 'is' for you.

Yours,

Explorator E

Can anyone test?

 Hi Evil Person! I've been told that anyone can test. That's not true. I'm not just anyone. I'm a tester. I've trained. Please set the record straight.

Chuck

Dear Chuck,

I get in to trouble sometimes because I say that "Anyone can test".

Note that I haven't described what I think 'test' means. But some people will immediately take offence at this statement because they already know what 'test' means.

And note again, that I didn't use the word 'professionally', but some 'professional' people involved in the testing process often read the word 'test' and interpret it as 'professional testing'.

Is that what you did?

When I look back over the testing I have done. I can see times when I tested more professionally than others. I noticed the following.

More professionally:

- I produced more written notes.

- I used tools to gain insight into the application.
- I created more screenshots.
- I knew what I wanted to do before I did it.
- I could describe the scope of what I covered in detail.
- etc.

Less professionally:

- My notes had less organisation.
- My notes tended to be written after the fact rather than before or during.
- I forgot to write stuff down. I didn't make any notes.
- I repeated myself.
- I couldn't say exactly what I had covered.
- I repeated myself.
- I got bogged down in areas without realising I was getting bogged down.
- I couldn't say why I was doing something.
- etc.

The simple fact is that anyone *can* 'Test'.

Anyone can do anything.

Anyone can build a table.

I built a table. It wobbled. It looked ugly. It took far too long to build. It would have been cheaper for me to have bought a table in a shop. I eventually threw my table away, and did buy one from a shop, so it was waste. But I built a table. And I learned that I build tables badly.

Anyone can do anything badly. Particularly without training or experience. Hopefully that does not describe you.

You need to be able to test better than 'anyone' off the street. And be capable of demonstrating that you can test better than 'anyone' off the street.

If you are confident that you can, then simply challenge the person, saying such disturbing things to you, to a "Test Off" where you sit down and 'test' an application.

If you discover that you aren't better than 'anyone'. Then work at it, until you are.

Better than 'anyone', but not as good as I can be yet,

Improv E.

 **I don't want to settle for 'good' testing.**

What is Sanity Testing and why should I care?

 What is Sanity Testing? When should I do it? How does it differ from Regression Testing?

Anon

Dear Anon,

Sanity is a cultural phenomenon. If someone holds the same set of beliefs as you, then they are sane. If their beliefs differ in an 'insane' way, then they are 'insane'. Often we don't recognise 'sanity' because we don't know what beliefs we actually classify as 'sane'.

We only recognise this classification of 'sane' and 'insane' beliefs, when someone holds an opposing belief and either: acts according to that belief, or states that belief out loud.

We can then judge them as 'sane' or 'insane'. But not everyone shares the same classification, which makes it a cultural phenomenon.

We have multiple cultures: family, team, work, personal, friend, legal, etc.

These can have different classifications of 'sane' and 'insane'. This allows us to behave in a 'sane' way with our friends, but the same behaviour would be classified as 'insane' at work.

Sanity testing then is: when we compare the system's statements of its beliefs, and the system's actions, to an agreed model of 'sane' statements and 'sane' actions. The model of 'sane' is the one that we, the team, agree upon. Sometimes in advance.

In the real world, when a person is classified as 'insane', they are prescribed 'rest' and 'talking cures'. In the software world we take a different approach.

In the software world: we kill the system, pull it apart into tiny pieces, engage in invasive surgery that we don't even know will make the system sane. Then quickly put the system back together again, try to start it up and bring it back to life (we call this execution), and then subject the system once more to our 'sanity' test. Woe betide the system that fails such a test as it is forced to go through a continual process of death, dismemberment and revivification.

This differs from 'regression' testing, because 'regression' testing has a different model. That model uses a classification of 'evolved' and 'primitive' to guide its belief investigation.

Sadly our cure for both software conditions is the same. A barbaric dismemberment, followed by disembowelment, leading to internal organ re-arrangement, and ultimately execution for reanimation.

Hope that brightened your day,

Barber E

Can I measure programmer quality using bug count?

 If a tester was asked by his QA manager to gauge a programmer's quality in terms of the number of bugs he creates while developing a website application, what steps does a tester need to take? I need a good answer which could satisfy the manager's need of gauging a programmer's performance through some or other metrics?

Anon

Dear Anon,

Ha! You josh. Clearly no manager would ask such a thing.

And if they did, my answer to you would certainly not satisfy the manager's claimed need.

The steps I would take are:

1. Laugh
2. Say "You can't be serious"
3. Say "No"
4. Laugh
5. Say "You can't threaten me"
6. Call Human Resources
7. Defend yourself until help arrives

If your manager wants to do this, then that is their madness. That is their job. Those are their windmills.

Part of your job requires you to decide which requests are sensible for you to take responsibility for, and which requests are so lacking in redeeming qualities that they should be bounced back immediately.

Other people could probably list 'nice' processes for doing this.

I'd recommend using words such as "No", "Never", "You're mental", "Not my job", "I think you'll have to do that" and "No".

Or you could take the route of automating the request. That might be fun. You could build a tool that takes a list of developer names (for this manager you might want the list to contain the names of developers on the project) and randomly sort the list into 'best developer'. Estimate the time it will take to build this tool as the same length of time that you estimate it will take you to find another job.

Bye.

Your always helpful, automatization recommending,

Uncle E

What is a Program Test Manager?

 What is a 'Program Test Manager'? I think every year new positions are made up just to confuse the real workers, but someone thinks they are recruiting for this position. I guess if you don't know that you are one then you ain't one, but I'd still like to know.

Anon

Dear Anon,

I don't know what a 'program' test manager is.

I know what a 'programme test manager' is. A 'programme test manager' is the fall guy for the 'programme manager' when the 'programme manager' delivers the system to the 'programme test manager' and the 'programme test manager' can't make the system work. Then the 'programme test manager' is the person that the other people in charge of the 'programme' blame.

Did you mean 'programmable test manager'? i.e. someone who will do whatever the upper level management team ask? And whom they can blame for anything?

It might be that your organisation has decided to create the management hierarchy from hell. And split the system into 'programs' that are individually test managed by a 'program' test manager.

Hopefully you'll move over to micro-services and then the 'program' test manager will have less responsibility than the 'real' workers and you'll finally have someone that you can boss about and blame.

I'll let you into a secret though. 'They' do create new positions to confuse the real workers. And not just every year. Every chance that 'they' get. And 'they' do this so that you keep your head down, and don't pay attention to the organisation. 'They' want you focussed on what you do. 'They' want to make it as complicated as possible for the 'real' workers to understand how a 'project', or a 'team', or a 'department' works.

Because 'they' know that if the 'real' workers ever figure that out. Then the 'real' workers would realise how much power they have and start changing things.

And that can't be allowed to happen.

Yours,

Agenda Test Manager Evi

Tell me about ad-hoc

 Tell me about ad-hoc!

Anon

Dear Anon,

I'm not sure you grasped the 'question' concept. You see the aim is that you ask about something you don't know, in a way that models weakness, then I answer with mocking.

See, what you wrote was a command. "Tell me...".

A question might read "Oh gracious evil one, I don't know what ad-hoc testing means, can you please enlighten me?"

Did you spot the obsequiousness? And the question mark?

So let me tell you about ad-hoc.

Google[7] definitions tell me that it means "created or done for a particular purpose as necessary." And its use has grown massively since 1950, either because population has grown massively (I did not compare the Google graph to a population graph), or because we do more things for 'particular purposes as necessary' now, or for some other reason.

Regardless, things for particular purpose.

And that means intent.

---

[7]https://www.google.co.uk/webhp?q=adhoc

Have you heard people call some testing 'ad-hoc', but they didn't mean 'for a particular purpose', they meant 'doing stuff' and they meant it in a derogatory fashion?

Now perhaps those people didn't understand what the testers were doing. Perhaps they didn't ask. Perhaps they observed a process, but not seeing what they associate with a test process (scripts, cases, etc.) they assumed it was 'stuff'.

If the process had no intent, and it was not for a particular purpose, then it was not ad-hoc.

But what if that was its purpose? What if intentlessness was their intent. What if they were channelling Eris, the Goddess of Chaos, what if randomness was their aim. Then it would look as though it was not ad-hoc, but it really was.

We have to learn to ask questions, and model processes so that we can understand them. Only then will we identify how appropriate they are for a particular context, and how 'ad-hoc' they are for the purpose they are used.

And we have to test with intent.

Hail Eris!

Who invented Liquid Soap?

 Who invented Liquid Soap and why?

Jim

Dear Jim,

I don't know.

Alan

PS. Please read my answer to 'What is Sanity Testing?'

 If "system testing is a necessary Evil" then "Evil testing is a necessary system".

Why do we have labels?

 Evil Tester, going back to the dawn of testing time... why oh why do we have labels? Regression testing, functional testing, penetration testing. Do we (the testers) need this? It's all testing isn't it? Maybe for those that don't understand our craft? Maybe for that never ending search of common language? Oops, more than one question in there.

Davey

Dear Davey,

I have labels on my plugs so that I know which plugs go in which games console. Seriously, you think they could have standardised, but oh no: "I'm an Atari Jaguar, I need a different display adapter from a Sega Dreamcast otherwise people will get confused".

And that's why.

When you own the name, you control the marketing.

When you control the marketing, you control the brand.

And if you control the brand, you get the budget.

Yup. This all comes down to cold hard cash.

Penetration testers get paid a bucket load of hard cash. Functional testers do not.

Sure. Its all 'testing', but then 'testing' doesn't cover it all, so really 'testing' is the wrong word for it 'all'.

And, more than half the time 'penetration testing' isn't testing. Its running tools that check for known versioned exploits. Can we say the same thing about 'functional testing'?

Labels become a problem when we use them, believing that other people interpret them in the same way. After all, "Regression testing" is not "testing" (it's a whole 11 characters bigger for a start[8]).

Labels can help shortcut communication when we have a shared understanding of what we mean by the label. And remember, we do not need that to be universally shared. We just need it to be shared among ourselves.

The hard part is remembering when you move between groups, which vocabulary you need to adopt, to avoid being identified as "one that can see[9]".

---

[8]My reviewers perform project roles in a 'test' capacity. This makes them incapable of reading a statement of fact without questioning it. One such reviewer claimed the count of 11 was true only if we counted spaces, and therefore made the case that there were in fact only 10 extra characters. The dictionary definition of character supports this view "a printed or written letter or symbol", "a symbol representing a letter or number". Of the top 5 results that Google returned for my search "online character count", only 1 of the 5 tools I tried agreed with the dictionary and my reviewer (which is a pity, had none agreed then I might have ignored the comment entirely). Also, in Regular Expressions, Dot '.' matches 'any character' including space. What a quandary. All of which just goes to show that ambiguity is present in the simplest of statements, and you should always have testers review your manuscript.

[9]http://www.imdb.com/title/tt0096256/

I can tell from your question that you have yet to be initiated into the secret order of "The Tester", otherwise you would already be aware of our Craft's "Ultimate Common Language" and would not worry about "The Outsiders" (those that do not understand our Craft).

I am not prepared to initiate you.

But I am prepared to tell you a secret which will allow you to survive in all of the many disparate groups that comprise "The Outsiders".

Don't use the labels.

Tell people what you mean, and tell them what you are going to do, using normal dictionary words. Words that have not become overlain with a discipline's interpretation.

For example, instead of "I'm going to do some penetration testing", say, "I'm going to run tool X with configuration Y to see if we are vulnerable to exploits A through G".

This will work, but will not lead to acceptance. "They" will know that you are not one of "Them" because you are not using their shared language.

But, as I always say. "Better a quizzical frown, than being hunted down (by skull faced aliens who actually control the planet)".

Yours,

33rd Degree Crafty E.

How do you invent?

 How do you find a good way to invent something?

Wolf

Dear Wolf,

The easiest way to 'invent' something is to build something without looking to see if it already exists. This explains many of the libraries and frameworks that exist in the world.

Clearly we would not class that as a 'good' way.

Another way might be to bring together a committee and discuss it for a long period of time. You are almost certain to bring in to existence something that has never existed before, since committee thinking is rarely focussed on a particular purpose and is often focussed on generic situations which do not actually exist. So while you may bring into existence something 'new' it is likely to be impractical and unusable.

I would not class this as a 'good' way.

Sometimes people invent things by accident. This often happens in chemistry and engineering. But in software we typically class these things as bugs. And while we may have brought something new into existence, we often don't want it.

I'd suggest that you focus on a problem, and if you can't find anything else that helps you solve that problem, and if you can't find anything you can tweak and tailor to solve that problem, then you set about creating a solution.

The important thing though is to drop your invention when necessary. For example, when :

- something equally good comes along that is maintained by others, and it is cheaper and easier for you to use their 'thing' than your 'thing'.
- you no longer exist in an environment which has the problem that your 'thing' solves.
- you have expanded the 'thing' to the point where it becomes hard to maintain, and it doesn't generate the funds required to maintain it. Either find something else, or strip it back to point where it solves the problem you need and consumes the time and cost that you can dedicate to it.

This might mean that you bring into existence something glorious, but which only exists for a short period of time. So be it. There will always be a problem around the next corner, and perhaps by giving up on this 'thing' you can create a new 'thing' to solve a new problem.

The hard part is looking at the problem differently from everyone else, such that you can see a way to solve it.

Hope that helps,

E in Stein

Difference between a guru, mentor and expert?

 What is difference between a testing guru, mentor and expert? Please also, how to find a learning plan and certifications to become the one with highest salary?

Yam

Dear Yam,

Wow. So many marketing words.

Guru has so many negative connotations, since almost anyone can call themselves a 'guru' and have a flock of disciples. But lets assume that 'guru' means teacher, and a teacher that is generally 'influential' or 'well known'.

A mentor is generally someone more experienced than you who gives you advice.

An expert is someone who is supposedly very knowledgeable or skilful.

I only use words like 'expert' and 'mentor' in marketing literature, and I only expect to be labelled with those words by conferences when they want to sell tickets to the conference by claiming to fill it with world renowned experts, gurus and mentors.

 Dear Conference Organizer

Throughout this book you will notice that I do my career no favours. It seems as though I've just alienated the conference organizers. But here's the thing. I was talking about all those 'other' conference organizers. Not you. You wouldn't do that. 'They' might. Those other ones. Not you. I didn't mean you. I meant 'them'. You know who 'they' are. Right. Yup. 'Them'.

All three words can be used to describe someone that talks to you, but doesn't do anything. Much like I'm doing here. I'm passing on information. I'm pontificating on topics. I'm not actually 'doing' anything. And I'm not demonstrating any capability or ability to actually do anything. So all three words can apply to someone who talks but can't do.

And that's why the words have a bad reputation. And why there isn't much difference between them, as words.

But there can be a big difference between them in your life.

Categorise the people who you have learned from as gurus, to you. But don't tell them that, because of the negative connotations in the words. Just thank them and tell them what you learned from them.

Categorise the people who you can go to for advice, that you trust, as mentors. But don't tell them that, because of the negative connotations and the implied responsibility that you have put on them. Instead, thank them for their help, and take responsibility for the implementation of their advice i.e. don't blame them if you fail when you apply their advice, take responsibility and learn, and then decide if you ever want to go back to them for more advice.

Categorise the people who demonstrate skills in an area as experts. But don't tell them that, instead, ask them "How" questions so that you can improve your expertise in the areas for which you admire them.

I don't think there are any general rules for which of the three has the highest salary. Although I suspect the more fraudulent they are, the higher the salary they manage to gather. Gurus typically have the higher salaries. Particularly if you take it to the extreme of creating your own religion.

I suspect however that you don't really care about the role distinctions. I suspect you just want to improve your skills, and that the path of the 'expert' is the path for you. So practice. Learn. Ask question of the people that you identify as gurus, mentors and experts. Study and improve.

Hopefully, by developing and demonstrating your skills, and learning to sell your experience and expertise, you'll increase your salary.

I can tell you what doesn't work though. Writing a book. That won't boost your salary. Nope. Don't do that for salary. It might mean that some people describe you as a Guru, or as an Expert, and it might mean that you can better sell yourself as a Guru or an Expert, but names don't pay the bills.

Being paid for skills, pays the bills.

Hope that helps,

Careers Advisor Mister E

Evil Tester and The Headless Browser

Is 'Test Automation' a waste of time?

 Is test automation a waste of time?

Anonymous

Dear Anonymous,

Thank goodness someone asked about automating. I was afraid that I wasn't going to be able to cross promote my other books[10] and training products[11].

Certainly engaging in activities to automate processes can result in wasted time. Sadly, so can many other activities in testing:

- writing 'scripts' that require maintenance with every system change.
- writing 'test cases' in advance that you will never 'execute'.
- writing documents that no-one will ever read.
- *to list but a few.*

We must endeavour then, to minimise waste across our entire test approach.

---

[10]http://compendiumdev.co.uk/page/books
[11]http://compendiumdev.co.uk/page/online_training

Fortunately that is one of the aims of effective automating. (In fact of effective *anythinging*.)

Instead of wasting time testing a system that has been installed incorrectly. We could instead automate the installation and execution process so that we know the system is installed correctly prior to us testing it.

Instead of wasting time setting up data to test against. We could instead automate the generation of data and population of the system with said data.

Now in some environments, neither of the two examples above, would be considered waste.

If our 'testing' demonstrates that the system has not installed correctly then that might be viewed as an effective use of our testing. Or is it? Perhaps we could find a way to automate the reliable checking of an effective install faster and more reliably than the 'testing'.

If we view the entry of 'data' as 'testing' because we are checking that the system allows us to enter said data, then isn't that an effective use of our time? Perhaps. But perhaps we could automate the data entry, and also automatically check that the system has accepted it correctly. That might give us more time to do even more testing.

Certainly it is more likely to be wasteful to attempt these automated actions in environments without the skill to do so. Certainly it would be wasteful if the tools and approaches were incredibly expensive and more time consuming than performing the action without the aid of an automaton.

In any event, waste becomes contextual, and any generic answer I could give, would have to be "No".

Your helpful handy Auto Mate,

Mister E.

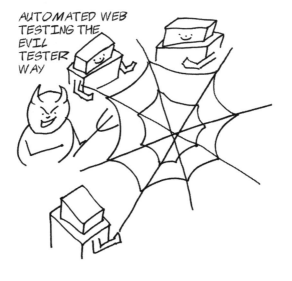

AUTOMATED WEB TESTING THE EVIL TESTER WAY

 I'm not Evil, I'm necessary.

Most common project failings?

 Evil Tester, what is something that fails the most in projects?

Lupi

Dear Lupi,

Wow, that's a hard one.

At least to be specific. That would be hard.

Here are some easy possible answers:

- Communication
- Process

Actually that's probably it, since you could model any system as a set of communicating processes.

Is one more important than the other though?

Does one contribute to failure more than any other?

If a process is bad, and impacts the viability of a system, then the rest of the system knows that because of its communication. If the system doesn't know that then it is a communication problem because we were not communicating the right things to allow us to maintain the viability of the system.

So I guess I have to say communication.

And now I feel bad. Because that is so generic, so woolly, so vague, so in-actionable and so intractable.

Guess what we have to do?

We have to take responsibility for, and own, the communication that we find ourselves part of.

In order to avoid falling prey to that big vague monster, we have to communicate well. Communicate using words that we understand. Communicate using words and phrases that clearly represent our intent.

We have to ask questions (a form of communication), to check if 'they' have understood what we tried to say (a form of feedback).

If we do that. And we do that well. And if everyone did that. Perhaps it is less likely to fail.

Did that make sense?

Yours,

Communiqu E

Is retesting a subset of regression testing?

 While searching an answer, regarding the difference between regression testing and retesting, I found that, regression testing is, testing all the test cases (both failed and passed) of a build after a new build has released. Retesting is testing only the failed test cases. My question is, can we say that retesting is a subset of regression testing?

Ana

Dear Ana,

We could say that "retesting is a subset of regression", and what would we have to believe for that statement to be true?

- Retesting means testing only the failed test cases.
- Test cases exist.
- Test cases can 'pass'.
- Test cases can 'fail'.
- We can test only 'failed' test cases.

If you can believe those things then yes, you can say that "retesting is a subset of regression".

I don't believe those things.

Do I use the phrase 'regression testing'?

On occasion. Even though I believe that the phrase has no valid meaning. So I instantly regret it, and then have to say what I mean.

I don't believe that systems 'regress'. I believe systems 'are'. I believe systems can exhibit behaviour that we don't want. I believe systems can exhibit behaviour that we don't want and which we have seen the system exhibit before. But I don't call that regression.

I test systems to find out information. New stuff. Stuff I didn't know. Stuff I thought I knew, but which my testing has demonstrated I had a false belief about.

For example, if we could login to the system, but now can not login to the system. Is that a regression? Or have we merely exposed a false belief that we held about the system?

I'll go for the latter.

When I use the term 'regression' testing, I'm thinking of approaches which are designed to confirm existing beliefs. Or rather, when they succeed and do not report an error, they offer no new evidence to make me doubt my existing belief. In some environments I might describe this as 'testing all the test cases (both failed and passed)'.

When I think of 'retesting', I also think of attempting to confirm existing beliefs. And, in addition, since I'm 'retesting' (testing again) I will be attempting to find out new information about the system. In effect, executing 'test cases' which I haven't executed before.

I try not to use the phrase 'regression' testing because I don't know what other people mean by that term.

I do use the phrase 'retesting'. At least, I did. In the future I will avoid the phrase 'retesting', because I was not aware of the connotation you provided in the question.

In the future I will probably just say 'testing'.

Hope that helps. And thank you. You helped me.

E.

 Not all testers are evil, just the good ones.

Which is the best test tool?

 Which is the best tool to help me test? And why is preference given to the experience letter rather than one's skills?

Myers

Dear Myers,

The best tool to help me test is my brain. I then use that to help me find other tools.

Generally I look for tools that help me:

- observe,
- interrogate,
- manipulate.

Observe means that I want to see more deeply into the system. I want to notice stuff that I might not otherwise see. By using a tool, I can have the tool observe something while I go off and observe something else, and the tool can alert me if it spots something I've asked it to monitor for. And I can go back and review to see what it has observed.

Interrogate means that I want to drill down into an observation and see what's what, at a level I haven't told the tool to monitor, or a level that I need to learn how to interpret. Or look into for a specific investigation, rather than an ongoing activity of 'seeing'.

Manipulate means I need to change something in the system. Generally at a level that the system doesn't expect or support. I might want to manipulate values in the database. Or I might want to manipulate an HTTP request the browser sends to the web application. I use tools to do that.

If you have a specific activity in mind e.g. observe HTTP traffic, manipulate a MySQL database, interrogate the obfuscated JavaScript code; then the tool I use is [insert name of generic internet search engine so as not to imply that one search engine is better than another], coupled with a well written query which my brain has helped me craft.

I'm often motivated to find tools because my brain has had enough and said "I hate doing this, find a different way!" or "I want to do this, and these clumsy human meat fingers are incapable, find a new way!" or something similar. By allowing my brain to pay attention to the signals my brain puts out, my brain can alert my brain to take action.

Much as I'd like to recommend "The One Tool", I can't. It does not exist. And I'd love to recommend "My Brain" but it works for me, and probably isn't as good as other brains, and probably isn't what you need. So the tool I'm going to suggest for you, is your brain.

Build it up. Develop it. Let it learn. Listen to it. And it will serve you well.

And as to why preference is given to the experience letter rather than skill. Well, if you were a lazy hiring manager what would you do?

Would you go through a practical audition based interview that required you to understand the skill set in advance and have the requisite ability to grade that skill in comparison to other people?

Or would you rather read an experience letter and check the spelling of a tool or skill you had been told you needed?

Yup. A lazy manager will go for the letter, and we can either:

- Don't worry about it and apply for roles where they look for skills. Develop our skills so that we build competence, and our confidence, such that we can demonstrate our skills on demand.
- Pad out our experience letter with buzzwords arranged to look like sentences, but make no sense when you read them because they are just collections of buzzwords separated by punctuation and conjunctions; safe in the knowledge that the lazy manager isn't going to read them as sentences anyway and is just going to scan them for the buzzwords.

Yup. Good choice. I'd do that too.

Yours, in a slightly less motivated mood now,

E-man.

How to interest people in testing?

 Hi Evil! Could you please give me some tips on how to get my colleague testers interested in testing? Actually they don't know much about testing, and they are not full time testers (they do the programming too). They were assigned with testing activities by the boss. Thank you in advance, Lal

Dear Lal,

Why are you interested in testing?

What makes testing interesting to you?

I assume that everyone is the same as me until proven otherwise. This 'otherwise' is usually proven very quickly when I ask them about their collection of small plastic religious iconography. At which point I quickly change the topic of conversation to testing.

I then describe and demonstrate what I find cool about testing the system we are working on.

The technologies and decisions we've made, and the interesting risks that have resulted from those decisions. I'll describe the challenges I face when attempting to identify if those risks have manifested in the system or not.

I'll describe the wild things I learn while testing the system. The new tools I master: to observe, and interrogate, and manipulate, the system at the different technological levels I've found the system to be composed of.

I might describe the challenges I faced customising the modelling and reporting I used to fit in with our System of Development. And the refinements I made to avoid 'waste', and the changes I've made from previous implementations to make it more effective for our project.

I might sit down with one of the current features and describe it from the point of view of a tester:

- the ambiguities that only become clear under a tester's gaze,
- the questions we have left unanswered,
- the risks we have implicitly accepted,
- the ideas we know we will explore, and how we came to find them,
- the possibilities that we might investigate, and why we might not,
- the tooling we might use, and the things we can't do if we don't.

Oh, the places we could go! If you are interested, and you can communicate your interest, then others will be interested too.

Sigh. Now I'm interested in your system, but it's not here.

Yours Interestedly,

I.E.

How do you test quality?

 How do you test the quality of a product?

B

Dear B,

I don't think I do test the quality of a product. I think I test 'qualities' of a product.

I test observations of those 'qualities', against models that I have made of the 'qualities' independently of the product.

And then I put the product into different states, allowing me to observe the product in different ways. I compare my observations of the product 'qualities' to my models of those 'qualities'. And when I see a difference, I can then offer commentary upon the differences between my observation and its comparison to my model.

Sometimes the commentary, after subsequent interrogation and investigation, will lead to me changing my model. At which point I can revisit the comparison of the system with the new model.

Sometimes I will have to convey my commentary to others. I have to refine my commentary into information, which I enter as feedback into the control mechanism of the System of Development that we are working with.

At least I think I do. At this point in time. In response to your question.

Vaguely yours,

E.

I'm not evil, I'm just doing WHATEVER it takes

Oracle database did not respond?

 Increasing the size of the Temp file of the Oracle database, the database did not even respond after restart. What was that?

Moz

Dear Moz,

Yeah. I know. Seriously.

What was that all about.

Databases!

Right! Am I right! Yeah. I'm right. I know.

Seriously. What was that?

Yours,

Admin E

 I'm not Evil. I'm doing this for your own good.

What's in your Test Tool Utility Belt?

 What do you keep in your Evil Tester Test Tool Utility Belt?

Vernon

Dear Vern,

It's your second question, so I feel like I know you. I feel like I can call you by a familiar colloquial name: 'Vern' or perhaps 'Vernie' or 'V'.

It almost feels like we're buddies.

Run away now.

No, Seriously. Good to have you back. So I can abuse you some more.

No, but seriously...

I used to have an imaginary belt. I did. I had a list of tools that I used, and I'd add new tools to the list when I encountered them. And I'd have another list of tools that I needed to investigate in the future.

But what I found was I spent a lot of time building a list, and less time using the tools.

I spent a lot of time investigating new tools, and less time learning how to effectively use the tools I had.

So I changed approach.

No lists.

No belts.

Instead, I identify an activity that I need the ability to do:

- Observe HTTP traffic.
- Create a file of test data from a Regex.
- Manipulate HTTP Form submissions before they reach the server.
- etc.

Then I ask *<insert your favourite search engine here>* "How X?", where X is the identified activity.

This means my 'tool' list is maintained by everyone else in the whole world (how's that for a bit of effective delegating). And all I have to do is work out what I need to be able to do.

And, sadly, that's the hard part.

The hard part is not finding tools, and making lists of tools, and learning how to use tools.

The hard part is figuring out what you need to do, to add value to your test approach.

So I'll tell you how I do that.

I look at my model of the system and I see which parts I'm not observing, or manipulating, or interrogating. I try and work out what risks I'm not testing for, because of that. Then I work out which of those risks I want to target. And I go looking for a tool to help.

And here's another thing.

Once I have a tool. I learn what it does. Because it probably does more than I need it to do. So I look to see if any of its features are things that I can see value in doing.

Having said that. I do have a tool belt. For mobile testing. Filled with sim cards of different sizes, and sim adapters. Because "I'm Batman"[12].

Yours,

Secret Identit E.

---

[12]From every Batman film ever.

Why do we test?

 An evil, but simple question. Why do we test?

Jools

Dear Jools,

Why? Why? Why do we ask why?

"Why?" is a question that targets beliefs.

If I answer you, then I'm just telling you what I believe. Why do you care what I believe?

In "The Gestalt Approach", Fritz Perls wrote:

> If we spend our time looking for causes instead of structure we may as well give up the idea of therapy and join the group of worrying grandmothers who attack their prey with such pointless questions as "Why did you catch that cold?" "Why have you been so naughty?"

What would you gain from my answer?

Ah, but if you had only asked "How?"

"How do you test?"

That would have been hard to answer.

I would have had to dig deep. I would have to codify my approach so that I could communicate it.

And you could have followed up, each step of the way, "When you say you do X...":

- What happens when you do that?
- Who cares about that?
- When would you do that?
- How specifically do you do that?
- How else could you do that?

And I would have been in such a mess. I mean I'd learn a lot about my approach to testing, but I don't think I'd find it so easy to answer, or so easy to dodge the question. Would you?

But when you ask "why?", I can answer without thinking: "Because the system is there to be tested."

How many definitions are tautological?

- What is performance testing? Testing the performance.

How many beliefs are tautological and without foundation?

- Why do we do performance testing? To test the performance of the system.

How many practices are the same?

- How do you do performance testing?
  – Erm... I just use tool X (i.e. I don't know)
  – Well... I <insert explanation here> (and then you can ask more questions to explore my expertise, or lack thereof)

People seem to love "The five Whys?[13]".

The portable TV is dead. (the problem)

1. Why? - Is the battery dead?
2. Why? - I think Bob used it all day yesterday.
3. Why? - Because he's an idiot
4. Why? - Because he watches daytime Soap Operas.
5. Why? - Because he claims he needs 'break' time away from everyone.
6. Why? - sorry, you are out of Whys and I could go on all day with this particular belief chain.

And yet people use this technique.

Why? I don't know, perhaps it works on everyone else, but not me.

---

[13]https://en.wikipedia.org/wiki/5_Whys

Why? I don't know, perhaps everyone else interprets "Why?" as "How?" and answers that question instead.

I try to only ask "Why?", when I want to know someone's belief chain.

Why do you ask why?

What question could you ask instead? How would that have triggered a different answer?

OK. I think I dodged the question.

Good night all,

Mr E lusive.

The untold story of the Test Plan

Why are some testers called QA?

 Dear Evil Tester, Why are some testers called QA? Is there a difference between a tester and a QA?

Dil

Dear Dil,

QA is used in Agile environments because everything has to be lean and fast. So people don't use real sentences, and if they write, they use SMS text writing rather than words. Also everyone is called by their initials rather than their names, except when the initials clash and then they use a nickname like "Test Boy" or "Ninja Dev Rockstar".

I have been told that QA is an Americanism. Apparently in America "Tester" is hard to spell, so they use the letters "QA". "QA" is also used as a verb, a department, and a role, because unambiguous clarity is paramount - I think that was the 9th amendment, or an old bylaw, or something.

Personally I find this unacceptable. "QA" should only be used in reference to Laphroaig's Quercus Alba Single Malt Whisky, or the process of "Quality Assurance".

As a tester, I'm not in the business of "Quality Assurance". I'm in the fear business.

And as far as I'm concerned the "QA" job starts with the CEO, and encompasses every other role down. If it starts with me, it ain't QA.

I think this stems from people buying a few "Quality" Management books and then not reading them. If they did, then they might realise that "Quality is everyone's job".

I personally refuse to take on the mantle of "QA" even to help those people whose lazy speak prevents them from writing or speaking the words "Tester", or "Testing". That is their problem, not mine. And like all minorities, I defend myself against derogatory and prejudicial labelling, so I do not allow people to call me a "QA", call my actions "QA" or call my work "QA". I understand that some people don't like it when I correct them. But I don't care.

I once channelled Theodor Geisel[14] and produced this little ditty that might help, I call it **"But do not call me a QA"**.

I do not like that name QA,
I do not like it, not at all, QA we do not say.
Tester, I do say,
It describes me bester, and how I play,
So it's far bester, to say tester,
And do not call me a QA.

Yours, in a hat,

Dr E.

---

[14]https://en.wikipedia.org/wiki/Dr._Seuss

What are the new trends in testing?

 What are the new trends in software testing?

Steve

Dear Steve,

This is great, I get to answer a question that when people read the answer in a few years, think I'm an out of date Luddite idiot.

Thanks Steve.

Of course, since no-one knows when I wrote these answers I could pretend that I'm back in the 80's and one of the new trends is how we react to changing requirements.

You see Steve, here in the 80's, we have our big hair, and shoulder pads, and we realised that requirements have a habit of changing.

And you know, changing requirements are a pain. You know what it's like. You've sat through the week long requirement document review meeting. And now the designers are 'designing' and writing the design document, and the architects are 'architecting' and creating the architecture document. And the testers are 'testing'.

'testing'

Writing a document, or multiple documents, with lots of test conditions, cross
referenced to test cases, where each test
case has a test script that tells the 'tester'
what to do to 'execute' the test case: what
buttons to press, what data to use, what
to look out for on the screen. Because we
'might' ask someone off the street to come
in and 'execute' that script for us. Of course,
we wouldn't, but we 'might', so it has to
be really detailed, just in case, you know,
because we 'might'.

And the programmers are 'starting' because they have a
fairly good idea of what they think the 'requirements'
are demanding. So they'll get started and change it later
when the 'designs' are designed and the 'architecture' has
been 'architected' and they'll ignore the 'tests' because the
'testers' deal with that.

Because if the programmers don't start, then you know
what they're like. They'll end up hacking into the pentagon,
or something technical that no-one else can understand,
because they're programmers.

Anyway. We write all this stuff down in big documents
that we have to review and discuss. And then. Would you
believe it. We learn something. And we have to change
the requirements. Which means we have to change all the
documents.

But the problem is that the testers have to go through every test, and every test script and change the same thing in a million different places. And that takes too long.

So the current trend will solve all that.

We call it "change control".

Basically. We 'control' the 'change' so that the 'change' doesn't happen.

We call it 'document sign off'. Every document has to be signed off. Including the test document. (And frankly no-one wants to read that. Blah blah blah boring.)

This means that we can avoid the impact of change on the 'test' documentation. And the testers can write all the test cases and scripts without having to worry that a requirement change will have a knock on impact on their detailed test scripts which anyone off the street *could* execute (but won't).

And our testers are so good, that they write many more test cases and test scripts than we could ever 'execute' in our lifetime. But that's good because now we have a measure of 'test coverage' which will tell us exactly what we didn't test, and then we have a number that will tell us the risk of going live.

The only problem is that the users keep wanting to change requirements. And so we have to have 'emergency' changes which we can make as small amendments to the designs and the architecture, and the programmers can change the code. Yes that's risky, but that's what the testers are for.

Unfortunately this creates an 'emergency' in the test team and they tell us they can't update all their scripts in time... and blah, blah, blah, boring. You know what they're like.

And we've just bought a new tool which the testers can use to 'record' their test when they 'execute' it, and then we'll be able to play back that recording when the programmers make changes and best thing is that the testers don't need to understand anything about how the tool works. Its like 'magic'. The testers call the tool 'shelfware'. Since the internet hasn't been invented yet, I can't [insert your favourite search engine name here] it and see what that means.

Anyway. This is all working out.

The project is estimated at five years. We're only into year two and I suspect I'll be promoted in a year, and I will have moved companies by year four, so I don't know if this will work yet.

But we're on track for a successful launch in the future.

Yours,

Marty McFlevil

How do you talk at conferences?

 Dear Evil Tester,

You speak at a lot of conferences. How did you start and how can I do that?

Gary

Dear Gary,

Maslow's work presents us with a model of a hierarchy of needs. As each lower level need is satisfied we then work towards satisfying our next need. People use this as a model of motivation. You might want to position yourself on the hierarchy and see if your 'needs' can be met by talking at a conference.

Personally I don't use that model for motivation.

Some people are motivated towards a utopian ideal. The notion that they have stories and experiences that will help enlighten other people and help them move forwards in their lives and careers. If you have such a utopian ideal then perhaps talking at conferences is a step towards you manifesting your vision. Focus on your utopian goal and keep that in mind as you submit to conferences. Allow it to motivate you to take action.

Personally I don't use that model for motivation.

I used to attend conferences as a delegate because I wanted to learn as much as I could about testing. I still want to learn as much as I can about testing. So I still enjoy conference talks that provide me with actionable advice, experience and ideas. Some of that advice may stem from the speaker's need to create their Utopia. I don't know. I don't focus on their motivation. I focus on what I can learn.

But learning wasn't the motivation for speaking.

I remember attending a conference and becoming so annoyed at the misinformation and the single-minded interpretation of other people's experience that flew in the face of my experience. I remember speaking to other delegates who were swayed by the speaker's talks and were about to embark on courses of action which they felt were the only path open to them, now that they had heard it from an expert; courses of action which I knew there were alternatives to. Courses of action that I thought were more effective, but I wasn't an 'expert' so I could not sway them.

That is what motivated me to talk at conferences.

I was not prepared to pay to listen to 'opinions' presented as 'the only way' and as 'facts' and 'inevitable outcomes'. I still wanted to learn, but I wasn't prepared to put my cold hard cash down to front this propaganda.

I was not prepared to passively allow a vocal minority present a single view of testing. When I knew, and had experience of, other options.

Even if my voice wasn't heard by many, I wanted to have some alternatives out there.

I started to talk at conferences as a reaction. I was motivated 'against' a system, rather than towards a vision.

And I learned a lot by doing so. I learned to ground my talks in experience rather than opinion. I learned that when it was opinion, I had to state it as opinion. I learned that there are alternatives, especially to the approaches that I present.

I learned that it wasn't just about presenting 'the experience'. It was about the decisions we made that led to 'the experience', the lessons that we learned from 'the experience', the actions we took, and will take, based on 'the experience', and trying to present all of this so other people can evaluate and take what works for them.

Now I have become part of the vocal minority. I talk at conferences and I hope some people listening react to what I say, by standing up and putting their experience forward as an alternative. Then we can learn from them.

We need more alternatives.

When we have alternatives, and options, we have to choose between them.

Choices force us to take responsibility.

And we need to take responsibility for our testing.

Start by finding out what motivates you, and then you'll have no choice.

Yours,

Vocal is E

Can one be technical without knowing how to automate?

 Can one call himself Technical Tester, if s/he is not good at test automation (e.g. Selenium, Watir)?

Alek

Dear Alek,

One can call oneself, whatever one wants. That doesn't mean one can live up to the designation.

But in the context of "Technical Tester", yes you can. GUI automating can become a very technical subject. But you can automate the GUI without understanding the technical aspects of the application. You may not know the database or the architecture, you may not even be aware of the HTTP requests flying about.

Technical has a broad scope. Far broader than limiting it to just automating stuff.

I suspect a technical tester will learn to automate as part of their test approach because it helps them, and they are likely to learn one or two programming languages along the way. But if they stand firm and refuse to improve their ability to automate then they can focus on other technical skills. In fact, they have to, they have no other choice.

When a phrase has a contextual definition, as "Technical Tester" does, then it can mean pretty much anything. We get to choose what definition we live up to. Others get to choose how they judge us by their definition.

Wars have been waged over lesser things,

Uncle E.

Evil Tester uses Selenium WebDriver

 Do whatever it takes!

Essays

Wot! We don't want no stinking essays.

OK, call this the padding section or something. I don't care.

This is stuff I had lying about on my hard drive that I wrote when I was trying to make sense of the testing world.

It is no longer 'stuff' because I've re-written it. Yes. I did that for you. To make it more concise and readable. And to explain some of the mindset that lies behind the answers.

You can skip this section if you perform a week long exercise that involves you re-reading the letters and answers previously. And for each answer ask yourself one question:

"What would I have to believe, to answer the question this way?"

And if you can't do that, or aren't prepared to do that. (I wouldn't.) Then this section is for you.

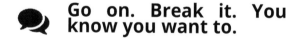 **Go on. Break it. You know you want to.**

What is Testing?

What is Testing?

Do you care?

Why?

- Do you want to know because you want to know where the limits of your job start and end?
- Do you want to know because someone asked you that question and you think you need to give them an answer?
- Do you want to know because you really like definitions of abstract concepts?
- Do you want to know because you need to pass an exam and give someone the right answer?

You might have a whole bunch of other questions - most likely you do since I only provided four alternatives to the "What is Testing?" question.

Questions I would rather people ask themselves include:

- What do I do?
- Why do I do what I do?
- What do I need to do now?
- What risks can I think of?
- How can we find out if this software can ...?
- I wonder if the software can still do that when ...?

But enough questions. Let me provide a simple answer to the first question "What is Testing?"

I don't think that such a 'thing' as "Testing" exists. Conversationally, a normal person might say something equivalent using the word sequence:

- "There is no such thing as testing"

And while that might not help you pass your exam, and it fails as a definition, and 'they' probably don't want to hear that answer, it might help you figure out where your job starts and ends.

Regardless, the above answer provides comfort and guidance to me during times of trouble.

If I ever find myself in a mess and think "What is Testing?" I can politely answer myself "There is no such thing as testing, figure out a better question to ask". Or "Stop hallucinating, concentrate on what you see happening now, figure out what to do next."

If I had an actual answer, and if I knew what a thing called testing looked like then I fear that I:

- might never look at the testing thing differently.
- might think that as a "tester" I couldn't do anything that didn't look like the testing thing.

Over the years I've come to believe that my job involves looking at things and processes and concepts differently.

I want the freedom to make stuff up, to pull in resourceful concepts as required, and the freedom to do what it takes to achieve the identified needs of the projects I work on.

I don't find the question "What is Testing?" helpful. I care:

- what preconceptions other people might have about my role and their expectations of me and people like me ("Testers").
- about the processes we use to identify, mitigate, and make manifest, risk.
- about making what we do efficient and effective.
- about agreeing actions and who will take those actions now.
- about a whole bunch of stuff.

And I test, because I care.

I just don't care about questions like "What is Testing?".

Do you? Why?

PS. I think I managed to avoid all mention of reification and e-prime. Did you notice?

PPS. If you don't know what 'reification'[15] means or what 'e-prime'[16] refers to, then look them up.

---

[15]https://en.wikipedia.org/wiki/Reification
[16]https://en.wikipedia.org/wiki/E-Prime

Unconventional Influences

 I submitted this as the supporting paper for my Keynote to Eurostar in 2012 therefore, no-one has read it and this is the first time it is been properly published. Which is a pity, because I think it is really rather good.

This time. I think I'll start with a rhyme.

The future of software testing requires you
to take responsibility for what you do,
and harness the things that make you you.

Your influences and experiences make you unique,
so you can speak from your heart (when you speak).

You will take responsibility, this writing demands.
The future of software testing is in your hands.

Sometimes I get worried about the future of software testing.

I see people getting heavily involved in standards and methodology frameworks, things that seem to change incredibly slowly, and ignore the feedback from the world around them.

I worry that people who adopt them, choose to bind themselves to historic moments on other people's evolutionary time-line.

I worry because I don't believe the world of software testing will improve until everyone involved in it, takes responsibility for their unique piece of it.

I don't want to see a world of homogenised, interchangeable 'testers' that all speak a high level language laden with ambiguity.

I want to see a world populated by software professionals. Individuals, who take responsibility for what they do; who can bring in new ideas, and can add unique value.

Perhaps it's just because I'm getting old. And when you get old, you are allowed to get grumpy, that's one of the trade-offs for grey hair. Young people don't know this, because they haven't had the "Laws of Ageing Handbook" through the post yet.

I get concerned because it seems like too many people are squandering their uniqueness.

Everyone is unique. We know this, we have unique DNA, we were all brought up in different ways. Even identical twins raised by the same people could not occupy exactly the same space at the same time, so they had different experiences. Everyone is unique.

So why the urge to homogenise? To talk the same? To do the same things in the same way?

I want to see more mutation in our communication. Ideas which change as they spread. Ideas which survive only because people take meaning from them and pass the meaning on anew.

So why the urge to homogenise? To talk the same? To do the same things in the same way?

Our uniqueness means that we all have the opportunity to harness our unique influences and use them to add the value that only we can. Everyone can add mutation to the testing DNA.

I know that some people don't think they have anything unique to add. They are wrong.

Some people think that unique means 'new and completely unlike anything else'. If you are one of those people and you're worried about it, then don't.

A unique and different slant might be just what someone else needs to hear to change. Your unique slant might help someone understand something that they had heard a dozen other teachers say without really grasping it.

Everyone has a unique perspective on the situation. Everyone can talk about their unique experiences and explain what they think worked and what they think didn't, what conclusions they have drawn, and what experiments they are going to try next. And they can do it in their own words.

Everyone has unique influences they can draw on to open up new possibilities for themselves or the people they communicate with.

Everyone has life lessons, learned from different environments, which they can transform into a mutant strain of testing DNA and unleash it upon the world.

The secret is that you are allowed to use your own words. You assimilate the lessons and learning from other influences. And you own the forward communication of them to other people.

Make a decision about how best to communicate your learning. Don't rely on a call to authority to make your point. If it is a quote that resonates, then quote the quote, and say who said it first. But the fact that someone else said it, won't sell the depth of meaning that you took from it.

You don't have to say that you remembered words of wisdom from the "My Little Pony" cartoon: "Maybe that's our special talent! Arguing!", and therefore you want to change the structure of the team meetings so that you explore more dissenting positions. You don't have to mention "My Little Pony", and you don't have to quote "My Little Pony".

Assimilate. Communicate the lesson you learned. Use your own words and talk from your heart.

And here is the real secret.

When you use the influences that are unrelated to software testing. You have to take responsibility for the assimilation. No-one else can. They are your influences. And that helps you take responsibility for your testing, because you start to own how you think about testing.

You'll start to make choices that seem obvious to you (because of your influences) that didn't occur to other people.

You'll have to use your own words to explain those choices because other people won't have the context to understand your influences, so you'll start to take responsibility for how you communicate testing.

When you do this, you'll know that you won't have bound your ideas about testing to moments in the past on someone else's evolutionary time-line.

You'll be building your own.

And I'll worry less.

References:

- My Little Pony, Episode 17, Series 1, "Stare Master" by Chris Savino. Script transcribed by Alan Back,
  - http://www.equestriadaily.com/

Selected Influences:

- Ross Ashby, "Introduction to Cybernetics[17]"

---

[17]http://pespmc1.vub.ac.be/ASHBBOOK.html

- Stafford Beer, "Designing Freedom"
- Charles Fort, "The Complete Books of Charles Fort"
- Robert Anton Wilson, "Quantum Psychology"
- Dr David Bourland Jr. "To Be or Not: An E-Prime Anthology"
- Alfred Korzybski, "General Semantics Seminar 1937"
- Herbert A. Simon & James G March, "Organizations"
- Richard Bandler, "The Structure of Magic"
- "Horton Hatches The Egg", Dr. Seuss
- "The Lorax", Dr. Seuss
- "Scrambled Eggs Super!", Dr. Seuss
- "Oh, the places you'll go", Dr. Seuss

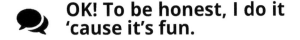 **OK! To be honest, I do it 'cause it's fun.**

Slogans

 A version of this text was posted on Evil-Tester.com in 2008[18]

I always thought the slogans would prove the most controversial part of EvilTester.com - more controversial than the cartoons, and more controversial than the name Eeeevil Tester. (You do have to say it like that, otherwise you take it far too seriously.)

So after putting these slogans in the text, with no explanation, I now present some reasons as to why the slogans exist.

And note... I regard this set of reasons as the 'serious' set.

"I'm not laughing...at 'you'!"

People take testing *way* too seriously.

I take it *waaay* too seriously at times.

In the past I took it *waaaaaaaaay* too seriously.

These slogans act as a reminder, to me, to loosen up.

To make sure that I can laugh at myself and my mistakes, so that I can learn from them more quickly.

---

[18]http://blog.eviltester.com/2008/05

I still take things seriously. But in a different way than I did before.

> "I'm sure it seems as though I'm Evil. But it's only because I care."

and

> "I'm not Evil, I'm doing it for your own good."

When I moved into testing, some people I knew could not understand why I made that move. I had the skills of a perfectly capable developer, and yet I moved into testing.

I did that because I cared.

In fact I cared too much.

I cared enough to adopt the identity of a quality policeman.

I cared enough to pursue quality with the same gusto that others pursue "World domination".

I *did* do stuff for *their* own good.

Now I try not to.

> "Now I do it 'cause it's fun"

Oh dear, I can't seem to switch my 'Evil Tester Sloganiser' off!

I do not want to adopt those traits any more.

These slogans remind me not too.

And they have the benefit that they make me laugh... which has the benefit of helping me remember them... and if I ever find myself heading towards that fixed and dogmatic type of state or emotion in my work life again, then the 'Evil Tester Sloganiser' kicks in with an EvilTesterism and stops me.

"I'm not Evil, I'm Necessary."

When I got into testing it did bug me that people would call 'testing' a necessary evil. *I later learned that those people also thought words like 'thinking', 'planning', and 'learning' were necessary evils.*

I remember scribbling the reversed statement "I'm not necessary. I'm Evil." during a 'what is testing' thinking session.

I added that little 'spurious' note into my more 'lofty' notes on testing because I really wanted to find different ways of doing 'testing'.

Many of the things that I did as a tester, I did because they *were* 'Necessary' or because they *were* 'Mandatory':

- Scripts before execution
- Xrefs to requirements

- Test Scripts so detailed that a trained monkey could execute them (provided the monkey could read English - no doubt seconded from the Infinite Monkey Project[19])
- ...I used to have so many of these type of things.

Those little notes got me thinking about what else I could do, when I did not have other words to explain it.

And even now the notion of "Eeevil" generates a state, a mindset, a view point, that can help me test that little bit differently very quickly.

A humorous state. A Mischievous state. A sneaky state. A "well what if I just... oops... wasn't me... quick leg it!" state.

You probably have your own trigger words. Identify them. Use them for your own benefit.

"I'm just doing WHATEVER it takes."

Prior to learning the concepts of "Exploratory Testing" or "Context Driven Testing" all I had was the nagging thought that 'there had to exist *better* ways of doing this stuff'.

And that also contributed to the concept of "Eeevil".

Diverting from the 'happy' path and taking the left hand path.

Leaving the script and going tinkering.

---

[19]http://en.wikipedia.org/wiki/Infinite_monkey_theorem

Doing some misdeeds to the system...

- Pushing and prodding it.
- Sticking it with a pitchfork or two.
- Gently roasting it over a roaring hellfire.

"Eeeevil" provides me with a rich set of metaphors, and they help me test. I guess some people use the term 'negative' testing for that.

"Of course I'm not Evil... Do I look Evil?"

I spend a lot of time improving my testing skills, re-assessing my thoughts about testing and incorporating models, approaches and belief systems from other disciplines to help me expand my 'goodness' as a tester.

Sadly, the better I became, the more distance grew between me and the 'traditional', 'best', 'right' or 'good' ways of doing testing.

What other word could I use other than "Eeevil"?

And unfortunately after too many years of studying hypnosis, and cultivating long hair and a beard, some people may think I look slightly Eeevil. That is their choice, people will judge, people will generalise, people will assume, we all do; testers need to do train themselves out of that.

"Go on. Break it. You know you want to."

But, you protest, we don't break software, it is already broken.

Well, it probably isn't even 'broken'. Broken suggests that it was working, then you did something, now it doesn't work. With software, it probably never worked. Just no-one noticed.

But that doesn't mean we can't try.

Remember, we're trying to build an attitude here.

Go on. You know you want to.

"Not all Testers are Evil... Just the good ones."

Ha. Now come on, comedy gold.

It instantly activates my 'over-generalisation' alert, and I always avoid over-generalising.

Each of the slogans violate what Alfred Korzybski[20] called the "Is of Identity[21]". Korzybski wrote a book entitled "Science and Sanity" which presented some of his thoughts on abstraction, generalisation and sanity.

Robin Williams on "Reality...What a Concept" said "You're only given a little spark of madness. You mustn't lose it.[22]"

---

[20]http://en.wikipedia.org/wiki/Alfred_Korzybski

[21]http://everything2.com/e2node/The%2520%2522is%2522%25200f%2520identity

[22]http://www.rd.com/your-america-inspiring-people-and-stories/quotes-from-comedians/article28210.html

On the same track of the album, Robin Williams then went on to say "And they haven't figured out how to tax that yet" (although I think I just paraphrased him).

Anyway, words to keep close to your heart if you don't have any room for any EvilTesterisms.

Summary

- Draw your own conclusions.
- The slogans are for my benefit not for yours.
- Write your own slogans.
- Don't stop. Don't ever stop. And don't let anyone stop you.

Seriously, an Afterword

Most people won't get this far. You did.

So I can level with you. Seriously now.

If you think this was about making fun of testing then... you're partly right. But really...

 ...this was about taking responsibility, and creating a future that you want to be part of.

Sometimes we ask questions when we really don't know the answer, and we want help.

Sometimes we have no choice. We can't ask anyone. We just have to decide.

Try something.

Take responsibility.

Take action.

Create a future.

You will make mistakes. I guarantee it. You can learn from those.

If you succeed, and everyone says how great you are, you probably won't know why. And then you'll be annoyed when you go to your next job, do the same things, and everyone calls you an idiot.

Because you didn't learn from your actions.

The feedback you received caused you to do it again without thinking.

When you fail. You figure out why. And you do it better next time. Regardless of whatever anyone else says to you. You know you've changed.

Did you react?

Did you react to any of the answers?

I hope you did.

I hope you thought:

- Well that would be the wrong thing to do.
- Well... maybe...
- Ha! No. Do this instead.
- *something else*

I hope the answers entertained, but made you think about what you would do. I hope you have a better understanding of how you think about testing and how you would approach the work.

Provocative Therapy

The world of psychotherapy in the 60's and 70's was filled with experimentation. Really, really mad stuff. I mean really, dolphins! And empty chairs! And... well, you can look it up if you want.

And one thing they experimented with were systems. People systems.

You may have heard of Virginia Satir and 'Conjoint Family Therapy'? Working with families as systems, changing the whole system, not just the 'person with a problem'.

We need to learn systems. We test systems. We work in a System of Development. And we interact with bunch of people systems - teams, organisations, projects, etc.

When you learn systems theory and systems thinking, you will encounter the notion of feedback.

- Positive feedback - the stuff that tells us we are on track.
- Negative feedback - the stuff that tells us to change.

Positive feedback is important, but hard to react to.

Negative feedback is easy. We react to it. We do something about it.

A therapist named Frank Farrelly harnessed that and made it a foundation of something he termed 'Provocative Therapy'.

Therapy where he, the Provocative Therapist, provoked the client with 'negative feedback'. Very often these were statements of observed fact that the client didn't like (negative) e.g. "you spend more time maintaining your test scripts, than you do testing. Why don't they just call you a 'script maintainer' instead of a tester." Harsh huh. But truth hurts.

Why would he do that?

At a time when Carl Rogers was going all humanist and helping people 'actualize', why were some therapists insulting their clients?

Because, we respond to negative feedback. We react to statements of truth that we don't want to believe. We react to statements we want to believe are false. We react.

And in therapy, reacting would imply taking responsibility for an action. Dropping victim status and starting to take responsibility. A first step on a road to 'self-actualization'.

But why did a client sit there and be insulted? Because the Provocative Therapist used humour, they told jokes, they phrased things in a light hearted, jovial, manner. Humour.

Listen to Bill Hicks. Listen to George Carlin.

Humour can tell hard truths in a way that people listen.

I noticed early on in my career that in many project meetings I was in, where the project was in utter disaster mode, the testers were the only ones cracking jokes. It was a defence mechanism, because they knew that whatever disasters were happening in the project, they were pretty soon all going to come crashing down on the test team.

But it was also a way to tell hard truths in a friendly, honest, humorous way. Much like a Provocative Therapist.

I didn't know that at the time. I learned about Provocative Therapy later. And when I read "Provocative Therapy" by Frank Farrelly, I could relate to it.

Take testing seriously

The comedians I like take things seriously. So seriously in fact, that they will mock them mercilessly. Flay them till the skin comes off and we can see the rotten innards that allow us to see the problem and take action that makes a change.

I take testing seriously.

That's what this is about.

I take this seriously enough that I will mock it. I will mock the decisions we make. I will mock the decisions I make. I will work hard to improve.

And I know, that I still have a lot to learn.

And the things I think I know now, are going to fail me in the future. So I can't attach myself to them.

Honest observation does not come easily. But if we are serious about what we do then we need to step back, observe, and comment in a way that we will take notice and take action.

I tried to do that with these answers. Sometimes more clinically than others. But for each question, an external person had to build a model of the questioner:

- What would I have to believe to ask this question?
- What would I be going through if this situation were true?
- etc.

Then, find a few statements that could open up a seam in that model to allow the questioner to look inside and provoke a response.

I hope you take testing seriously enough to question your models of testing and recognise your 'absolutes' for what they really are: 'beliefs', and that when they fail you, and they will fail you, that you will accept the negative feedback and learn to adopt a new approach.

I hope you exhibit the requisite variety you need to survive and that you can evolve your models of the world, and explore the world in safety and armed with a cutting sense of humour.

When you do, you'll take responsibility for your testing, for your questions, and for your own answers. And you'll build a future that you can live in.

I also hope that you are not a despotic megalomaniac and that you recognise that you are part of system along with other people.

Are you a despotic megalomaniac?

Then please read Carl Rogers instead of Frank Farrelly.

Responsibility

Ultimately this, and much of my work, concerns responsibility.

Providing people with the skills, the techniques, the models, the motivation, the provocation, to take responsibility for what they do.

I hope you will.

 ## Be Good

Good and Evil are relative terms.

If you accept that, then words hold less power over you. Choose your actions well. Stop labelling them 'Good' and 'Evil'. Take responsibility. Build your own models. Do what you need to.

Do what you have to, to be the change you want to see.

Recommended Reading and References

When I was answering these questions, I would scan my bookcase for inspiration - mainly the book spines rather than the content. But occasionally I had to crack open a book to pull out a quote.

In this section I will list some of the sources that I drew upon.

I like to encourage people to 'go to the source'. Do read the references, but also track down the references mentioned in the references, and read what they were built on; that can lead to a surprising chain of study.

I will also list some of the popular culture references I mentioned in the text. I use the word 'popular' loosely since I'm not particularly trendy.

Recommended Reading for Software Testing

To improve our testing we need to study Software Testing. And when I look at my bookshelf to see what Software Testing books I still retain, I see many that I enjoy, but only a few I can recommend to 'everyone'.

I don't wish to overload you with testing books, since studying these will take time. Especially if you 'go to the source' for all of these books, and create your own interpretations and models of the material presented.

Software Testing Techniques

Written by Boris Beizer, this is the only 'technique' book I keep handy. And one of the few testing books of which I have multiple copies. There are other more popular books, but this appeals to me. Densely written, it requires study. But I think it presents some of the fundamental techniques in more detail than later similar books. When you read this you might get the impression that testing has something to do with Set Theory, Graph Theory and Computer Science. And you might think that you need to learn about those topics too.

Lessons Learned in Software Testing

Written by Cem Kaner, James Bach and Bret Pettichord. This is a book to dip in and out of. It benefits from three points of view which offer different perspectives on the same point under discussion. Experience based, it makes you think, and offers re-read value. The only other testing book, of which I have multiple copies.

How To Break Software, How to Break Web Software

Written by James Whittaker, with collaborator Mike Andrews. These books haven't 'aged' well. The software they use, and the tools are out of date. Which means that you will have to work to gain the value from them. As a study approach I suggest you make notes on the techniques, then generalise them to principles, then identify ways of implementing the technique with current browsers and operating systems.

What, is that it?

Seriously dude, there are so many books out there on Software Testing, you should read as many as humanly possibly. Really, I read everything I could get my grubby little hands on. But the ones I listed above are those that I re-read. The books that have little overlap with other texts.

In some ways, these books are a provocation to you.

When you read Beizer you might go "Whoah! There must be something simpler than this!". And there are many technique books, simpler than this, they just don't present the same level of detail or study value.

When you read Kaner, Bach and Pettichord you might think "Wha! I have to interpret this and decide what to do!" True, but there are other books that present templates and processes and approaches that you can adopt without thinking too much.

When you read Whittaker, I know you'll have to find 'new' tools and 'new' approaches to do what they describe. You will have to identify the aim of their technique and 'learn' how to achieve a similar result on your own system.

So yes. That's it[23].

"What! No books on automation!". Well, this was a book about 'testing', not 'automating'. But if you're interested I listed my favourite books on automating in the recommended reading section of my book "Java For Testers".

Other Non-Traditional Testing Books

I only know of two other 'non-traditional' testing books, which educate with a light hearted manner, and both I can recommend:

- "I am a Bug" - Robert Sabourin's Children's testing book. A funny, slim volume, with a deep heart, a light step and a lasting presence.
- "Cartoon Tester" - Andy Glover's compilation of testing cartoons. Funny, educational, and available from leanpub[24].

---

[23]You   can   find   more   books   listed   at
http://compendiumdev.co.uk/page/bookreviews
[24]https://leanpub.com/thecartoontester

Non-Testing References

These books were mentioned in the text, and I will offer some commentary as to why.

Science and Sanity by Alfred Korzybski

The massive tome that forms the basis of General Semantics[25]. A body of work that aims to make people conscious of the abstractions that we make and the models that we interact with. There are many other books which offer cut down, bite size versions, see also the Wikipedia entry on General Semantics[26]. A heavily influential book. Korzybski's "General Semantics Seminar 1937" provides a shorter introduction and summary of his work.

Introduction to Cybernetics[27]

Written by Ross Ashby. Cybernetics deals with systems, feedback and control. Ashby describes the notion of 'Requisite Variety' - the flexibility of response required by a system to deal effectively with the 'input' that the system receives. A notion worth its weight in gold when you want to write contextual test strategies that actually add value to your organisation, rather than introduce waste and re-use boilerplate.

---

[25]http://www.generalsemantics.org/
[26]https://en.wikipedia.org/wiki/General_semantics
[27]http://pespmc1.vub.ac.be/ASHBBOOK.html

Designing Freedom

One of Stafford Beer's Management Cybernetics books. Where he expands on Norbert Wiener and Ross Ashby's work to describe ways of building team and organisational communication processes to create a 'viable' system. A 'viable' system being one with the Requisite Variety to survive and thrive in an organisation. Something we might wish for every test team and department.

The Complete Books of Charles Fort

Charles Fort collected reports of anomalous phenomena. 'Stuff' that science could not explain, but that people experienced as fact. What I like about Fort is that he didn't just do a "Ripley's Believe it or not" and report on it, he added his own explanations. I get the feeling that he did this to 'provoke' - if science wouldn't explain it, he would, in the hope that science would acknowledge the phenomena and provide a rational explanation. I view him as an early provocative therapist.

To Be or Not: An E-Prime Anthology

Dr David Bourland Jr. developed the concept of 'e-prime' to try and find a fail safe way to avoid Alfred Korzybski's 'is of identify' where people get hung up on concepts and can't see them as abstractions and models, a process that Korzybski believed contributed to 'insanity' in its many and varied forms.

Quantum Psychology

I enjoy reading Robert Anton Wilson's books, and "Quantum Psychology" is the easiest one to recommend to testers. Written in 'e-prime', English without the verb "to be". Why? To avoid Alfred Korzybski's 'is of identify' and attempt to write 'objectively'. It provides a useful introduction to abstracting and 'e-prime'. I frequently write defect reports in 'e-prime', particularly when they deal with a contentious topic. (I even wrote a tool[28].)

The Structure of Magic

By Richard Bandler and John Grinder, this two (short) volume set of books presents a 'Meta Model', a model of the language structure that therapists use when questioning clients. Drawing heavily from Chomsky's linguistics, Virginia Satir, Gestalt Therapy and General Semantics. This is very practical way of modeling systems to question their assumptions and presuppositions. Something that testers do. I drew heavily upon this for my "NLP for Testers[29]" papers which provide an introduction to the meta model and its application for Software Testing.

Dr Seuss

I specifically want to draw your attention to "Oh, the places you'll go" and "The Lorax", which emphasise personal responsibility and continual learning to create the flexibility and requisite variety you need to survive the future. And

---

[28]http://www.compendiumdev.co.uk/page/eprimer
[29]http://www.compendiumdev.co.uk/page/nlp

"Scrambled Eggs Super!" and "Horton Hatches The Egg" which deal with 'doing things differently' from others and introducing variety into your thinking and processes.

Provocative Therapy

Frank Farrelly created a "Devil's Advocate" style of therapy which used humour and provocation to trigger a client into taking responsibility for their situation and leading to change. At points, the answers Evil Tester provides are intended as a humorous provocation which could lead to change.

Gestalt Therapy Verbatim

Fritz Perls, Gestalt Therapy books contributed to changing my views on using questions for change. Specifically how certain questions can target beliefs, and other questions can explore mechanisms. Both are important when we want to change behaviour.

Organizations

Written by Herbert A. Simon & James G March in 1958, I still think is one of the best books on team and organisational dynamics available.

Pop Culture References

The fact that these are 'references' does not mean they are not recommended. I love them. But they relate even more loosely to the act of testing than the recommended reading and are really listed to describe the popular culture references in the main text. These were referred to in passing rather than directly listed as references.

By all means hunt this stuff out. But do your research on-line first and make sure that our 'popular culture' tastes align first.

Consider yourself warned.

Cyborg, by Martin Caidin

I drop Martin Caidin's name into the ranks of Cybernetic luminaries like Ross Ashby, Stafford Beer and Norbert Wiener. Caidin's "Cyborg" novel was later adapted into the TV Show "The Six Million Dollar Man", and therefore no-one reads his "Cyborg" series anymore. The pilot episode of the TV Show was fairly close to his first "Cyborg" novel. But very dark for a Children's TV series - the hero's despair at his loss of humanity and his subsequent attempted suicide, the philosophising around 'what makes us human' - not really what kids want. Later episodes fixed this by adding springy sound effects when the hero jumped over high fences, having the hero jump over at least one high fence in every episode, and at least one super high speed super slow motion run. Every. Single. Episode.

The Wizard of Speed and Time[30]

Mike Jittlov's wonderful film. From which I paraphrased one of the answer sign off's, the original quote was "May All Your Good Dreams and Fine Wishes Come True". This is a great film. A film about a short film maker trying to make it into Hollywood big time by making a big budget short feature and getting ripped off by his producer. This plot was subsequently mirrored in Mike Jittlov's real life story. Also this film is an inspirational example of content re-purposing - using your original short films as part of a feature film movie about a movie maker who makes short films trying to break into Hollywood and make a feature film. I can't remember how many times I've watched this. I kept my VHS player simply to allow future watching of this film. Then YouTube happened. But I still have my VHS.

They Live[31]

John Carpenter's 1988 film about an invasion of skull faced zombie aliens. An invasion which completed successfully without anyone noticing, until we invent special sunglasses. And you should watch it, because we're all out of bubble gum.

Discordianism[32]

As described in the Principia Discordia[33], this is a constructed religion based around the Goddess Eris. I refer-

[30]http://www.imdb.com/title/tt0081766/

[31]http://www.imdb.com/title/tt0096256/

[32]https://en.wikipedia.org/wiki/Discordianism

[33]https://en.wikipedia.org/wiki/Principia_Discordia

enced this in one of the answers with a "Hail Eris!" sign off. I find Discordianism interesting to relate to testing because it is built around deliberate contradiction and humour. Testers need to contradict the system and the system paths during their testing, and they need to face the project with humour. A detailed description of the evolution of discordianism can be found in the book "Historia Discordia[34]" by Adam Gorightly.

Malleus Maleficarum

A question about metrics prompted me to draw upon the "Malleus Maleficarum", the 1487 text that provided the double bind mechanisms used in Witch Trials to allow an inquisitor to demonstrate that almost everyone was a witch. I decided to mutate the "Rituale Romanum" used in exorcisms to the "Rituale Exploro" and place it in the hands of an Indagator (latin for someone who investigates) as a means of combating the evil of misused metrics. Seemed like the natural set of metaphors to me, what would you have written?

Warren Zevon

"poor poor pitiful me" was a direct quote from Warren Zevon's first album.

Juggling for the Complete Klutz

This was the book, and bean bag set that I used to learn how to Juggle. I have subsequently gone on to teach over 50 people how to juggle. Poor poor pitiful them.

---

[34]http://historiadiscordia.com/

Pinocchio

I suspect people don't read Carlo Collodi[35], instead they rely on Disney's interpretation of the story of Pinocchio. The book certainly has more adventures, more death, more torture and moral lessons than the cartoon. Perhaps the most important lesson for testers happens very early on, when the experienced Talking Cricket (over a hundred years old), is battered to death with a hammer by the young puppet for attempting to raise valid risks and concerns to the young team member.

---

[35]https://archive.org/details/pinocchio00coll

Unrelated Reading

And one last book I would like to draw your attention to which, while not related to software testing, I think you might enjoy, on the assumption you enjoyed this.

How to Lengthen Our Ears

Written by Viscount Harberton. Did I just make that up? Bing it to Google and see. Perhaps I did. Perhaps I made up the husband of Lady Florence Harberton: the victorian women's freedom fighter who created the Rational Dress Society in 1881 and campaigned for 'Rational' dress for women cyclists (a short skirt worn over a pair of knicker-bockers), a form of fashion that frequently meant that she was barred from entering many a hotel and eating establishment. However, perhaps as an early english advocate for the use of the written spelling 'alright', Viscount Harberton deserves our attention. And then I won't be the only tester who has read this 'enquiry' into 'whether learning from books does not lengthen the ears rather than the understanding'. Partly a fulmination against putting 'literature' before 'experience', and partly a condemnation of the education act and the 1902 revision thereof with its emphasis on 'compulsary' and 'standardised' education. This book may, or may not, be found on archive.org (for those of you without a 1917 hardback copy handy).

Be whatever it takes!

About The Author

Alan Richardson is a test consultant. He tests things, and helps people test better. **He is not Evil**.

Alan helps people improve their ability to automate - primarily with Java, but has also worked with Ruby and .Net. He also helps teams improve their ability to test within an Agile environment, make their exploratory testing more effective and test to more technical levels.

Alan blogs at EvilTester.com[36], here he mainly writes practical articles on technical and exploratory testing.

Alan performs keynotes and tutorials at conferences worldwide. You can find his presentations and papers on his consultancy web site at CompendiumDev.co.uk[37].

Alan also offers online training[38]. And at the time of writing has on-line training courses for learning:

- Selenium WebDriver API with Java[39]
- Technical Web Testing 101[40]

---

[36]http://eviltester.com
[37]http://compendiumdev.co.uk
[38]http://www.compendiumdev.co.uk/page/online_training
[39]http://compendiumdev.co.uk/page/seleniumwebdrivercourse
[40]http://compendiumdev.co.uk/page/techweb101course

Alan wrote the book "Java For Testers[41]" which teaches Java programming from the perspective of writing @Test methods rather than applications. This provides the basic programming knowledge required to write code to automate the execution of other applications.

Alan maintains the SeleniumSimplified.com[42] website which has articles and tutorials on using Selenium WebDriver.

Alan also wrote the book "Selenium Simplified[43]" which taught basic programming skills and Selenium-RC.

Alan Richardson has over twenty years of professional IT experience: as a programmer, tester and test manager.

Alan works as an independent consultant, and he could be helping you right now.

You can contact Alan via his website:

- compendiumdev.co.uk/page/contact_us[44]

---

[41]http://javafortesters.com
[42]http://seleniumsimplified.com/
[43]http://www.compendiumdev.co.uk/selenium/
[44]http://compendiumdev.co.uk/page/contact_us

Made in the USA
Middletown, DE
12 May 2016